Prairies and Savannas in Michigan

Ryan P. O'Connor · Michael A. Kost · Joshua G. Cohen

Prairies and

Savannas in Michigan

REDISCOVERING OUR NATURAL HERITAGE

Michigan State University Press · *East Lansing*

∞ The paper used in this publication meets the minimum requirements of ANSI/NISO Z39.48-1992 (R 1997) (Permanence of Paper).

Michigan Natural Features Inventory

Michigan State University Press
East Lansing, Michigan 48823-5245

Printed and bound in China.

15 14 13 12 11 10 09 1 2 3 4 5 6 7 8 9 10

LIBRARY OF CONGRESS CATALOGING-IN-PUBLICATION DATA
O'Connor, Ryan P.
Prairies and savannas in Michigan : rediscovering our natural heritage / Ryan P. O'Connor, Michael A. Kost, and Joshua G. Cohen.
p. cm.
Includes bibliographical references and index.
ISBN 978-0-87013-845-4 (pbk. : alk. paper) 1. Prairie ecology—Michigan. 2. Savanna ecology—Michigan.
3. Prairies—Michigan. 4. Savannas—Michigan. I. Kost, Michael A. II. Cohen, Joshua G. III. Title.
QH105.M5026 2008
578.7409774—dc22
2008029517

Book and cover design by Sharp Des!gns, Lansing, Michigan
All cover images are used with permission from the photographer. Clockwise from upper left: White-tailed Deer by Dave Kenyon, Hill's Thistle by Bradford Slaughter, Monarch Butterfly sipping nectar from a Marsh Blazing Star by Dave Kenyon, Blanding's Turtle by Barb Barton, Birdfoot Violet by Dan Kennedy, Eastern Meadowlark by Jerry Jourdan, Prairie Coreopsis by Bradford Slaughter, Michigan Savanna by Ryan P. O'Connor.

green press initiative Michigan State University Press is a member of the Green Press Initiative and is committed to developing and encouraging ecologically responsible publishing practices. For more information about the Green Press Initiative and the use of recycled paper in book publishing, please visit *www.greenpressinitiative.org*.

Visit Michigan State University Press on the World Wide Web at *www.msupress.msu.edu*

Contents

Acknowledgments

No publication is solely the work of its authors. Numerous individuals contributed to this project in significant ways. The authors would like especially to thank Mark Sargent, private lands biologist with the Michigan Department of Natural Resources (DNR). His passion for grasslands and private land conservation has guided the DNR Wildlife Division's Landowner Incentive Program (LIP), which provided funding for this project in partnership with the U.S. Fish and Wildlife Service. The authors would also like to thank Susan Tangora, Michigan LIP coordinator, and Dan Kennedy, Christopher Hoving, Brian Piccolo, and Kevin Swanson, LIP biologists. Their tireless work to improve wildlife habitat for rare and declining species on both public and private land serves as an inspiration for others attempting ecological restoration. In addition, they also provided valuable editorial comments.

We are also thankful for the staff at the Michigan Natural Features Inventory (MNFI), past and present, many of whom contributed in some way to this project. Much of the history, classification, and current state of knowledge of prairies and savannas in Michigan was pioneered by Kim Chapman. We are indebted to him for his contributions and research. Numerous other individuals lent their expertise through extensive fieldwork, literature reviews, and abstracts. These include Dennis Albert, Patrick Comer, Susan Crispin, David Cuthrell, Yu Man Lee, Mike Penskar, and Mary Rabe. Dave Cuthrell also provided editorial comments. Additionally, Mike Penskar, John Paskus, and Pat Brown helped guide this project through many twists and turns.

Pictures bring to life natural beauty that words can only begin to describe. We are indebted to the numerous photographers who generously contributed images to this project, including Charles Peirce and Jerry Jourdan; Harold Malde and Chuck Pearson of The Nature Conservancy (TNC); Mac Deuparo of the Michigan Nature Association; Dave Kenyon, Christopher Hoving, Dan Kennedy, Brian Piccolo, and Robert E. Clancy of the Michigan DNR; Dave Brenner of Michigan Sea Grant; and Dennis Albert, Barb Barton, Suzan Campbell, Susan Crispin, David Cuthrell, Kile Kutcher, Mary Rabe, Gary Reese, Mike Sanders, and Bradford Slaughter of the MNFI. Doug Pearsall of TNC also graciously provided access to TNC photo archives.

Finally, we would like to thank MNFI administrative staff, including Pat Brown, Yu Man Lee, Lyn Scrimger, Nancy Toben, Sue Ridge, and Connie Brinson, for their assistance with budgeting, account management, equipment, and vehicles. This project would not have been possible without the help of Julie Loehr and the staff at Michigan State University Press.

Introduction and Purpose

This publication is a summary of information related to the history, classification, and management of prairie and savanna communities in Michigan. Information has been synthesized from a wide variety of sources, including peer-reviewed journal articles, practical handbook publications, published and unpublished field research, and historical and anecdotal accounts.

This book is not intended to be a comprehensive stand-alone reference, but rather to serve as an introductory user-friendly guide to prairie and savanna communities for citizen scientists and those with a general interest in natural history. Readers are encouraged to review publications listed in appendix 3 and the bibliography for more in-depth information related to the ecology, classification, and management of these fascinating parts of our natural heritage.

Historical Overview of Prairies and Savannas

A Living Legacy of Our Past

When immigrants settled in the Midwest in the early 1800s, the landscape was vastly different than today. At that time, savannas occupied over 10 million acres (4 million hectares) of the Midwest, and prairies covered a similar or larger amount of the region. With their open, aesthetic areas ideal for establishing towns and often excellent soil for agriculture, these landscapes became the setting for the first settlements in Michigan inland of the Great Lakes. Prairies and savannas are a legacy of our past, providing the inspiration behind the names of the very landscapes in which we live, places such as Oakland County, Prairie Ronde, and Oak Grove. This legacy surrounds us not just in words or historical accounts but in living remnants in our own backyard. Although once common in portions of the state, these unique natural communities have suffered severe declines and now occupy less than 1 percent of their former extent. This is especially evident of the "oak openings," a type of savanna known for stately, open-grown oaks, lush grass, and colorful wildflowers. Often mentioned in historical accounts of being "so characteristic of

OPPOSITE: Butterfly gardens are a popular way to enjoy native wildflowers and wildlife in urban and suburban environments.

Suzan L. Campbell

the Michigan scenery," oak openings have all but vanished. Remnants of many prairies and savannas remain, however, and continue to provide habitat for a unique array of plants and animals, many of which are found nowhere else. Threats to these species and communities are numerous and include changing land-use patterns, invasive species, and fire suppression. The need for conservation is great, but through rediscovery and restoration we can preserve this living heritage.

Although Michigan is generally thought of as a state dominated by forests, prairies and savannas made up a significant component of the circa 1800 landscape, especially in the southern Lower Peninsula. Because the state's northerly latitude and relatively abundant rainfall were ideal for trees and forests, prairies and savannas were concentrated in areas of the state that experienced frequent fires and sites with either very droughty or very wet soils.

What is the difference between prairie and savanna? In general, a prairie is commonly described as a grass-dominated community with less than one tree per acre (2–3 trees per hectare). In contrast, savannas have a partial tree canopy with prairie vegetation beneath. However, savannas are much more than simply prairies with scattered trees. Many prairies

TABLE 1. Prairie and Savanna Communities along a Moisture Gradient

	WETLANDS		UPLANDS		
	WET	**WET-MESIC**	**MESIC**	**DRY-MESIC**	**DRY**
PRAIRIE TYPE	wet prairie lakeplain wet prairie	wet-mesic prairie wet-mesic sand prairie lakeplain wet-mesic prairie	mesic prairie mesic sand prairie	dry-mesic prairie hillside prairie	dry sand prairie
SAVANNA TYPE		lakeplain oak openings*	bur oak plains	oak openings lakeplain oak openings*	oak barrens oak-pine barrens pine barrens

*Lakeplain oak openings can occur on both wet-mesic and dry-mesic sites.

tend to be dominated by grasses with a smaller component of forbs (wildflowers and other broad-leaved herbaceous plants), while savannas tend to be just the reverse, with a groundcover dominated by forbs and comparatively few grasses. Savannas range from having 1–30 trees per acre (3–74 trees per hectare), a maximum of approximately 1 tree every 30 feet (9 meters). Canopy cover can range from 5 to 60 percent, depending on the type of savanna. Other terms used in the literature for savannas include barrens, woodlands, and oak openings, all of which are lumped under the general category of savanna for the purposes of this publication. In addition to the amount of canopy cover, prairies and savannas are further broken into different natural communities by ecological characters such as soil moisture (table 1). More detailed information on the types of prairies and savannas can be found in the chapter titled "Prairie and Savanna Classification in Michigan."

OPPOSITE: Savannas are much more than prairies with scattered trees. Where the canopy creates filtered light conditions, wildflowers tend to be more dominant than grasses, especially in mesic and dry-mesic communities.

DURING GLACIATION

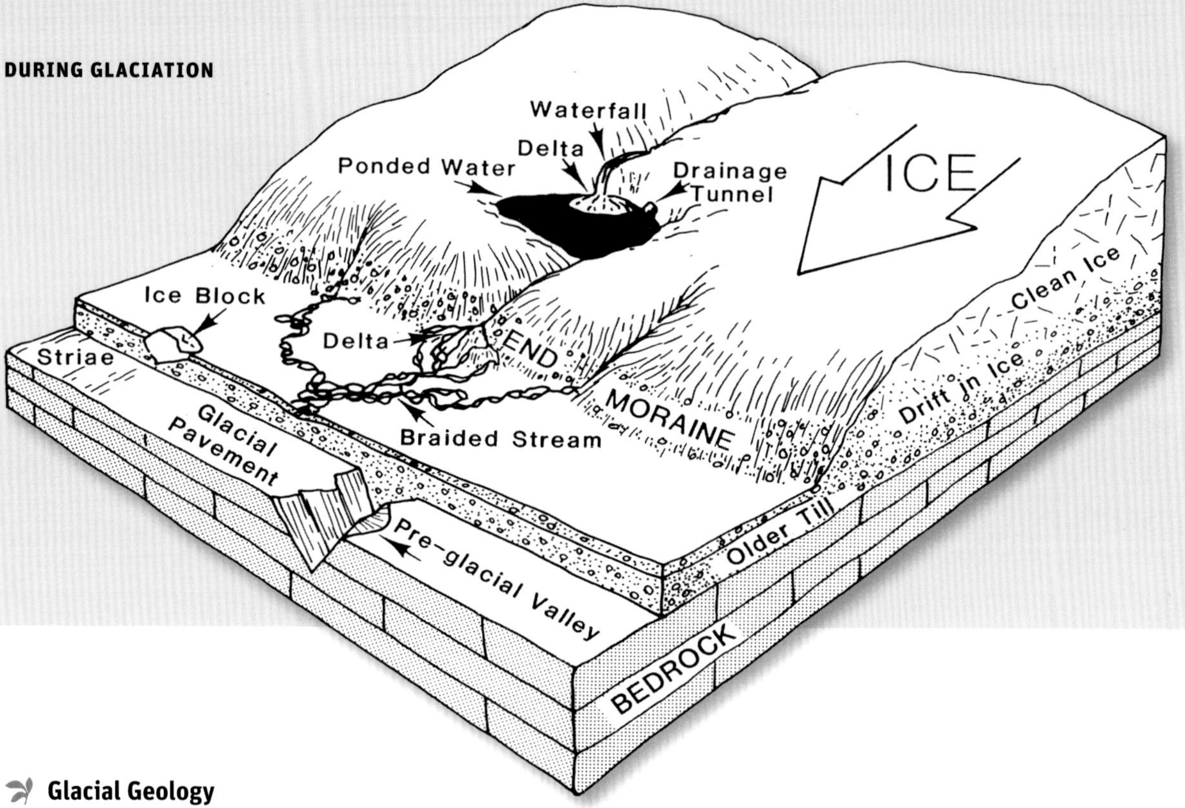

FIGURES 1 & 2. Advancing ice and melting glaciers shaped the landscape, leaving behind landforms such as outwash plains, moraines, kettle lakes, kames, and eskers. Reprinted from W. R. Farrand, *The Glacial Lakes around Michigan*, with permission from the Michigan Department of Environmental Quality, Office of Geological Survey, Lansing, Michigan.

Glacial Geology

The distribution of prairies and savannas in Michigan is largely dictated by landscape features and soils that were laid down by glaciers over 10,000 years ago. Advancing from northern latitudes, glaciers carried with them tons of cobbles and rock, which were pulverized into sand, silt, and clay under the weight of ice more than one mile (1.6 kilometers) thick. As the climate gradually warmed, retreating ice and glacial meltwater left behind new landforms of hills, valleys, and plains (figures 1 and 2).

AFTER GLACIATION

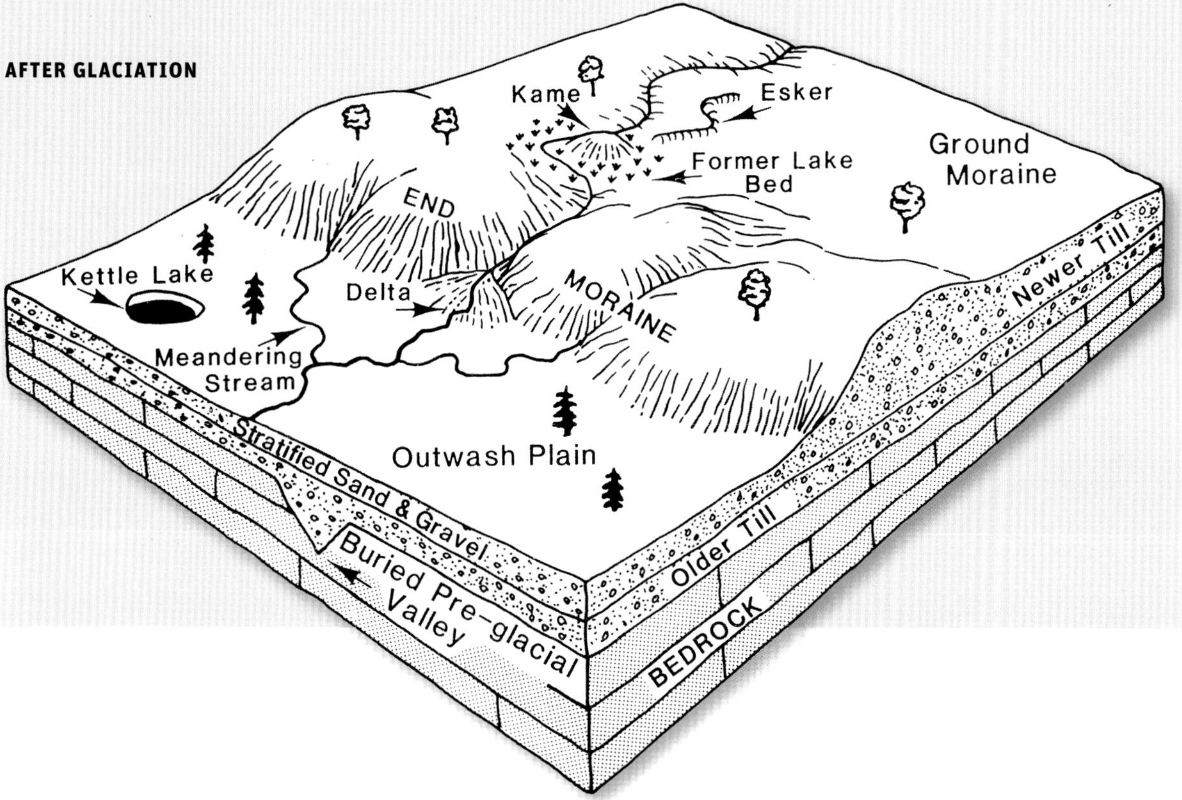

Many of these glacial landforms contain certain types of soils that support distinct communities or habitats. For example, dry prairies are often found on droughty, sandy plains left behind by glacial floodwaters. In contrast, lakeplain prairies in the Great Lakes regions are found only in areas where precursors to the lakes once stood, often at much higher levels than today. Lakeplains are characterized by sandy ridges where ancient beaches once stood and low swales of silt and clay, a result of fine sediments

that settled out of the glacial lake water. However, the majority of prairie and savanna communities are found in the interlobate region, a complex landscape of hills, valleys, and level plains that formed where lobes of glacial ice met.

During glacial advances, large lobes of ice advanced through preexisting Great Lakes basins. Originating from the areas now occupied by modern-day Lake Michigan, Lake Huron, and Lake Erie, lobes of ice spread across the landscape. Where these massive sediment-laden glacial lobes met, they left behind a landscape rich in topographic variation and biological diversity now referred to as the interlobate region. As the ice melted 15,000 to 10,000 years ago, massive hills of sediment called moraines were deposited along the retreating margins of the glacial ice sheets. Expansive level areas called outwash plains were formed as broad sheets of glacial meltwater transported and deposited a blanket of sand across large areas of the landscape. In the interlobate region in particular, a diverse landscape of hills and valleys formed. Linear, winding hills, termed eskers, formed from glacial streams tunneling through the ice. Steep, rounded, gravelly hills called kames derived from material deposited by giant blocks of stagnant ice. Finally, where rivers carried away glacial meltwater, valleys referred to as outwash channels formed.

These glacial features form a very heterogeneous landscape in the interlobate region that historically supported different types of prairie and savanna. Oak barrens developed on the most well drained and infertile portions of the landscape, such as drought-prone sandy outwash plains and the tops of sandy and gravely moraines, kames, and eskers. Oak openings formed on outwash plains, lakeplains, and moraines, where soil water-holding capacity and nutrient levels were slightly greater. Steep, south-facing slopes of moraines, kames, and eskers supported hillside prairie. Where soils were saturated in outwash channels along streams and lakes, a variety of open wetland communities developed, including wet prairie and wet-mesic prairie.

OPPOSITE: Oak barrens occur on flat, drought-prone outwash plains.

From a regional perspective, the majority of prairies and savannas in Michigan were located in the Kalamazoo and Jackson Interlobate regions, a broad swath of land stretching from Cass and Van Buren counties in the southwest to Oakland County in the southeast (figure 3). Other important regions for prairie and savanna include the droughty and infertile soils of the Newaygo Outwash in northeastern Lower Michigan and the High Plains region centered around Grayling. Dry savannas such as pine barrens can also be found in portions of the Upper Peninsula.

Prairies in a Savanna Landscape

In Michigan, savannas were historically much more common than prairies. In a 1932 soil survey of Branch County, the landscape was described thus: "The so-called prairies were not entirely treeless, but supported a scattered growth [of trees], consisting principally of bur oak [*Quercus macrocarpa*], . . . but the tree growth was not sufficiently dense to prevent the growth of heavy grass cover" (Moon et al. 1932, cited in Chapman 1984).

A summary of the General Land Office survey conducted in Michigan from 1816 to 1856 estimated that prairie and savanna occupied 7 percent of the state at that time (Comer et al. 1995a). Savannas accounted for over 80 percent of this total and formed the dominant matrix of open habitat (figure 4). When compared strictly with upland prairies, the historical acreage of savannas exceeded prairies by a factor of nearly 30 to 1. Savannas were also often much larger in size than prairies. With the exception of a few large areas of lakeplain prairie in the southeast and upland mesic prairie in the southwest, most prairies were small and were embedded in a much larger matrix of savannas.

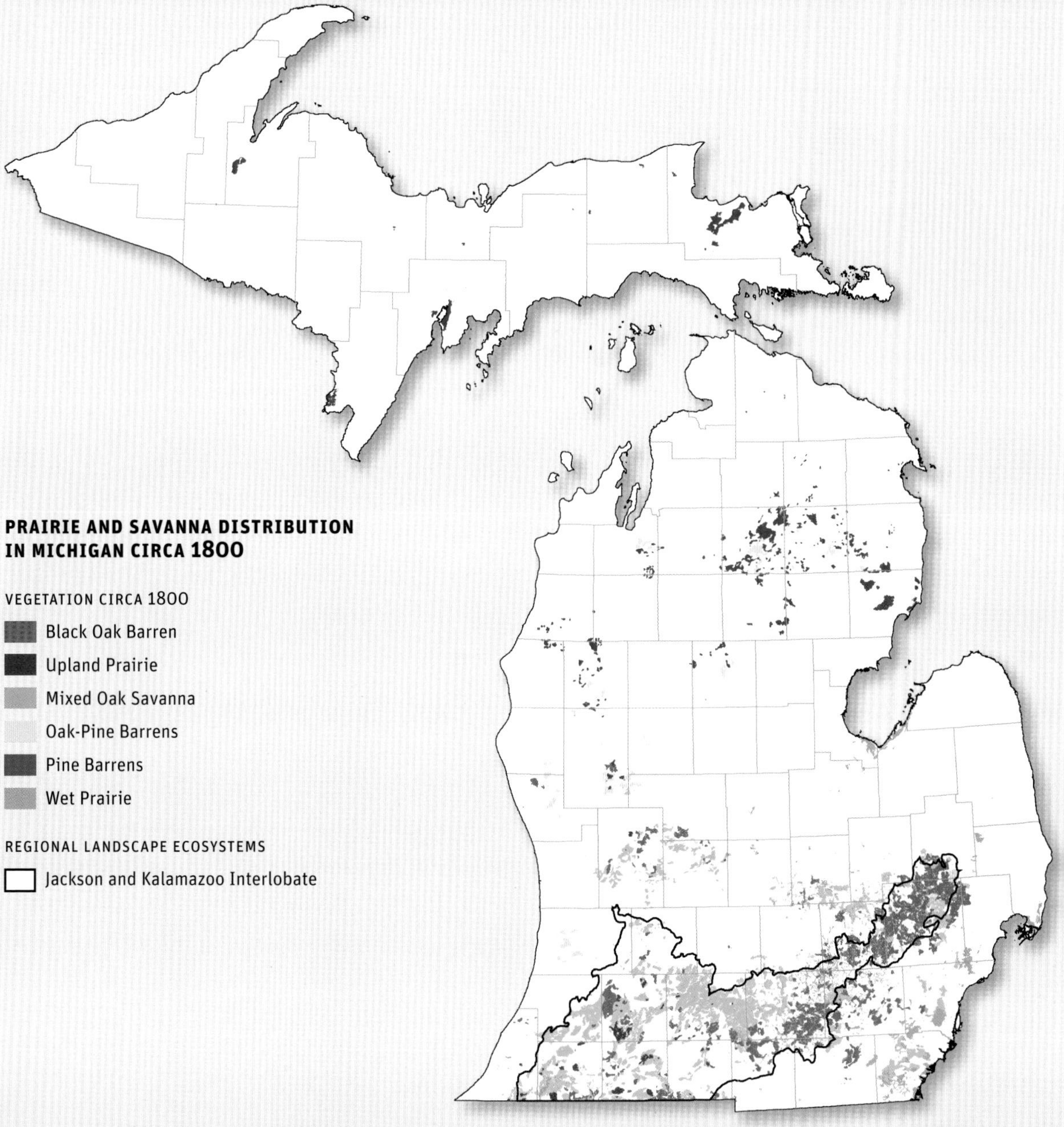

FIGURE 3. Circa 1800, prairies and savannas were concentrated in the Jackson and Kalamazoo interlobate regions, but smaller pockets could also be found throughout the state. Data sources: Vegetation circa 1800: Comer et al. 1995a; Regional Landscape Ecosystems: Albert 1995.

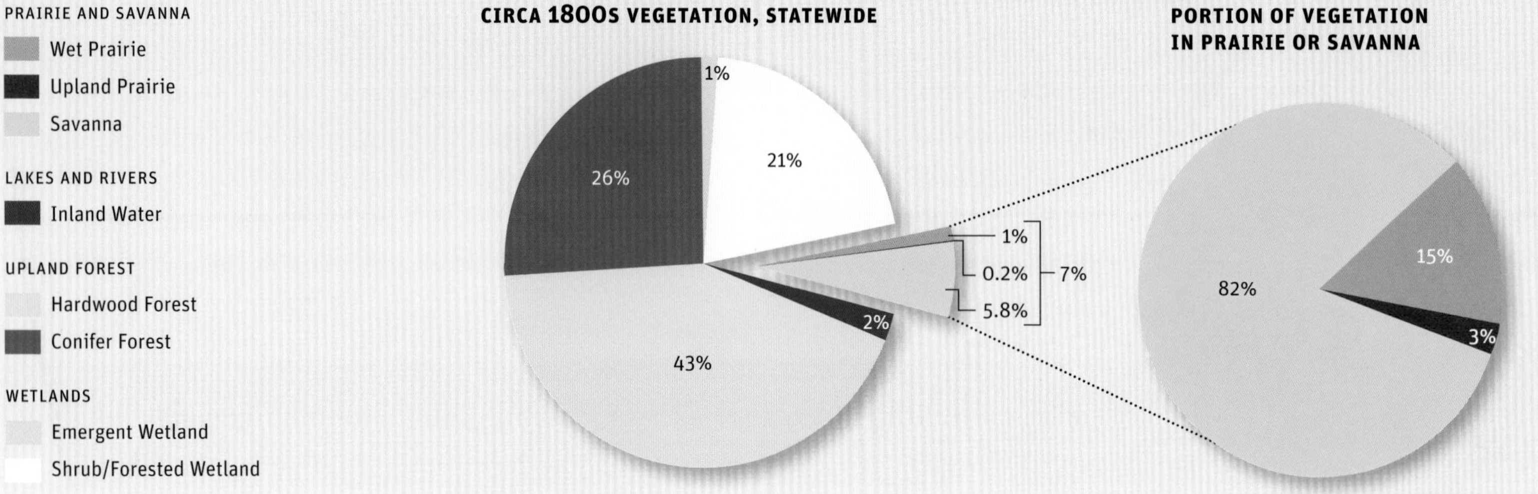

FIGURE 4 (ABOVE). Around the turn of the nineteenth century, prairies and savannas accounted for 7 percent of the landscape in Michigan. Of this, savannas comprised the vast majority.

OPPOSITE: Savannas were common in southern Michigan historically.

Ecological Processes

The defining character of prairies and savannas is their open canopy. With enough sunlight reaching the ground, prairie grasses and wildflowers flourish and provide the necessary structure and food resources for the associated wildlife community. Without natural processes to maintain an open canopy, trees and shrubs quickly dominate. As canopy cover increases, prairie and savanna species decline, and are replaced by more shade-tolerant plants. This leads to a wholesale change in community composition and structure for both plants and animals. Thus, maintaining an open canopy is critical to the functioning of prairie and savanna ecosystems. The primary processes that maintain open conditions are fire, drought, and water-level fluctuations.

Bradford Slaughter

FIRE

Historically, fire was the most important process that maintained savannas and prairies in an open condition. Fires burned more frequently in regions with a predominance of droughty level outwash plains, such as the interlobate and High Plains regions. Open wetlands that were a part of this landscape, such as wet prairies, were often juxtaposed with oak savanna, and when fire burned across the uplands, it easily carried across the adjacent grass and sedge-dominated wetlands as well. Fires in prairie and oak savanna communities burned off only fine fuel such as grasses, leaf litter, and dead woody debris. Large standing trees were rarely consumed in a fire, though intense flames might kill mature trees by damaging the outer conductive tissue with extreme heat. In general, fires in prairies and savannas were not the catastrophic crown fires now typical of fires in the large coniferous forests in the western United States. One notable exception is the jack pine–dominated forests in northern Lower Michigan and the Upper Peninsula. Jack pine (*Pinus banksiana*) is particularly prone to large, stand-replacing wildfires, and has unique adaptations to regenerate itself after fire, such as serotinous cones that are sealed with resin and open to release seeds only after being exposed to extreme heat.

LEFT: Showy lady's slipper (*Cypripedium reginae*).

OPPOSITE: Surface fires were historically common in prairies and savannas. Though these fires consume fine fuel, they rarely destroy mature trees.

Fires affect prairies and savannas in multiple ways. They stimulate grasses and wildflowers, while simultaneously limiting the growth of trees and shrubs. Fires also remove built-up thatch and expose mineral soil, facilitating the germination of small-seeded wildflowers. In the spring, blackened soil absorbs more solar radiation, rapidly warming the ground and effectively creating a longer growing season. In the prairie and savanna communities of southern Michigan, fire frequency, or how often a site burned, historically ranged from annually to every five years. The fire frequency at any given site was determined by a variety of factors such as topography, the amount and type of fuel, natural firebreaks, and proximity to other fire-prone ecosystems. Historically, drier communities (such as oak barrens and dry sand prairies) likely burned least often (every three to five years). In contrast, more mesic and dry-mesic communities (such as mesic prairie and oak openings) likely burned annually due to high annual fuel loads. Annual fires and their effects on the landscape have been noted in several historical accounts.

> The annual fires burnt up the underwood, decayed trees, vegetation, and debris in the oak openings, leaving them clear of obstructions. You could see through the trees in any direction, save where the irregularity of the surface intervened, for miles around you, and you could walk, ride on horse-back, or drive in a wagon wherever you pleased in these woods, as freely as you could in a neat and beautiful park. (Van Buren 1884, cited in Chapman 1984)

Historically, fires originated in two ways. Lightning strikes sparked periodic blazes, especially during dry thunderstorms. These fires might start small and smolder for days or weeks, only to grow into a larger fire when weather conditions allowed the fire to spread. However, fires were also deliberately set by Native Americans for a myriad of reasons, some of which included stimulating berry production, assisting with hunting by driving or encircling game, maintaining open landscapes for ease of travel and increased

OPPOSITE: Fires benefit prairies and savannas by setting back shrubs and tree seedlings, removing dead leaf and grass litter, and stimulating the growth of grasses and wildflowers.

visibility, and concealing escape from enemies. In part, Native Americans may have set fires because they also recognized that fires improved habitat, especially by promoting a fresh, lush growth of new grass that was more nutritious and palatable to grazing animals than the previous years' tall, coarse, dried litter. Fires also had the effect of maintaining a mosaic of habitats. An early explorer in Michigan noted both effects, and also described the important process of fire burning from the prairie into the surrounding woods:

> To-day, for the first time, I saw the meadows on fire. They are of vast extent, running far into the woods like the friths on a lake; and as wild grass, which they supply in the greatest profusion, furnishes the new settler with all the hay he uses for his stock, they are burnt over thus annually to make it tender. These fires traveling far over the country seize upon the largest prairies, and consuming every tree in the woods, except the hardiest, cause the often-mentioned oak openings, so characteristic of the Michigan scenery. (Hoffman 1835, cited in Chapman 1984)

Thus, fires created a mosaic of prairies grading into savannas and savannas grading into more closed-canopy forest. Changes in fire frequency caused this dynamic mosaic to shift, with more frequent fires opening the forest canopy, and thinning savanna trees. Conversely, and far more common following the settlement boom, less frequent fires allowed tree seedlings and shrubs to rapidly fill prairies and savannas, eventually forming closed-canopy forests.

OPPOSITE: Many early explorers such as Dr. Bela Hubbard, a companion of Douglass Houghton in the early 1800s, described the prairies, savannas, and lakes in Michigan with aesthetic appreciation and poetic language: "The variety so essential in a landscape, of woodland, glade and sheets of water, are here combined in a manner which seems the result of art."

In addition to noting the characteristics of prairies, savannas, and the fires that maintained them, early surveyors also expressed a deeper, aesthetic appreciation of the landscape:

> The variety so essential in a landscape, of woodland, glade and sheets of water, are here combined in a manner which seems the result of art, but which is not less truly inimitable. It is difficult to resist the

Charles Peirce

Charles Peirce

> impression that we are surveying an old abode of civilization and of tasteful husbandry. It resembles those exquisite pictures of park scenery, where the vision roams at will among the clumps of lofty oaks and over open glades, gemmed with flowers; while the distant woodland bounds the horizon, and velvet-skirted lake gleams upon the eye as it reflects the light from the open prairie. (Hubbard 1840, cited in Fuller 1928)

~ EXTREME SOIL CONDITIONS

Extreme moisture and nutrient conditions also contribute to ecosystem processes that maintain an open canopy by limiting tree and shrub growth. Droughty soils, which are often nutrient-poor, result in slow tree growth and an overall sparse canopy. Conversely, too much moisture also can inhibit tree and shrub growth. As tree roots grow, they respire metabolically, a process that requires oxygen from air trapped in soil pores. When soil is saturated, these pores are filled with water instead of air, and most trees have difficulty growing. Many herbaceous plants have specific adaptations that allow them to tolerate high water levels and thrive where most woody plants cannot.

Many herbaceous plants such as butterfly weed (*Asclepias tuberosa*) (TOP) are adapted to droughty soils; other wildflowers like fringed gentian (*Gentianopsis crinita*) (BOTTOM) thrive in wet soils.

Extremely wet soils, as well as highly acidic or basic soils, also limit the ability of plants to absorb nutrients. Most trees and shrubs are poorly adapted to wet sites with low nutrient availability.

As soil moisture and nutrient availability become less extreme, tree and shrub growth increases, and fire frequency becomes relatively more important in maintaining open conditions. Open canopies in both wet and dry sites are maintained by either waterlogged or droughty soils, respectively, in addition to frequent fires. In contrast, mesic sites depend almost entirely on annual fires to promote prairie and savanna vegetation, since soils are ideal for tree growth, and canopies quickly fill in without fire.

BIOLOGICAL FACTORS

Numerous animal species also played historically important roles in prairie and savanna ecosystems, sometimes being as or more important than frequent fires in maintaining grasses and wildflowers. In the Great Plains region, American bison (*Bison bison*) was one such keystone species, grazing preferentially on grasses and enhancing wildflower diversity, creating critical microhabitat through wallows, and boosting nitrogen cycling through excrement. Though bison were quite rare in Michigan and elsewhere in the Great Lakes region, herds of other large herbivores such as elk (*Cervus canadensis*) and, to a lesser extent, white-tailed deer (*Odocoileus virginianus*) may have had similar, though much less pronounced, impacts.

Beaver (*Castor canadensis*) is another keystone species credited with maintaining prairies, especially along streams, along wetland edges, and on lakeplains. Dams cause areas upstream to flood, killing trees and promoting growth of herbaceous species adapted to high water levels. Beaver herbivory further reduces tree survival within wetlands and adjacent uplands. Mound-building ants (*Formica* spp.) play a crucial role in the soil development of prairies and savannas. In addition to creating microhabitat, ants mix and aerate the soil as they build tunnels and bring nutrients to the surface. Mounds can easily be 10 square feet (1 square meter) in size, and because they take many years to develop, they are often found

Dave Kenyon

in areas that were not intensively farmed. Thus, the presence of large ant mounds is a useful indicator of prairie and savanna remnants. Ants are also the primary dispersal agents for many plants species, including violets (*Viola* spp.) and trilliums (*Trillium* spp.). Seeds of these species contain special sugary food bodies called elaiosomes. Ants collect the seeds, consume the elaiosomes, and discard the seeds in underground tunnels, where the seeds later germinate and establish new plant colonies.

The extinct passenger pigeon (*Ectopistes migratorious*) is also thought to have played a crucial role in maintaining savanna ecosystems. Roosting in oak trees by the thousands, they increased the fine fuel needed to sustain frequent fires by breaking branches and small twigs. Additionally, they may have helped maintain the dominance of fire-tolerant bur oak (*Quercus macrocarpa*) and white oak (*Q. alba*), by preferentially selecting acorns of other species such as red oak (*Q. rubra*) and black oak (*Q. velutina*).

Changes in Prairies and Savannas circa 1800 to Present

With the spread of settlers came radical and rapid changes to prairies and savannas. Naturally open sites with loamy soil were among the first areas chosen for farmland, and those areas not converted to agriculture were often selected as sites for towns, college campuses, and cemeteries. Fire frequency decreased as Native American populations declined, towns grew, and the need to protect homes and crops from wildfire increased. As more roads were built, the landscape became increasingly fragmented, and fires that did occur were far less widespread.

Even by the 1870s, this change was well under way, as described by Hubbard only 35 years after an 1837 expedition near modern-day Pontiac in Oakland County with the renowned Michigan explorer Douglass Houghton:

> The surrounding country seemed to our eyes far enough removed from the gloomy morass [surrounding Detroit] which wild imaginations had depicted it twenty years before. It appeared to me the most beautiful the sun ever shone upon. It was of the character then beginning to be classed as "openings," characterized by a gravelly soil and a sparse growth of oaks and hickories. I speak in the past tense, because, though the rural beauty of the country is still unrivaled, little remains of the original character of the openings. This is a result partly of the progress of cultivation, and partly of the thick growth of small

OPPOSITE: White-tailed deer and herds of other large ungulates such as elk are important parts of prairie and savanna ecosystems in Michigan.

RIGHT: White oak is an important fire-tolerant species of savannas.

Ryan P. O'Connor

timber that has covered all the uncultivated portions since the annual fires have ceased, which kept down the underbrush. (Hubbard 1881, cited in Chapman 1984)

The conversion from prairie and savanna to forest was astonishingly rapid. In many cases the change occurred within decades (25 to 40 years), with more mesic communities like bur oak plains converting even more rapidly. Often, the rapid conversion was due to the presence of abundant oak "grubs," clumps of stump sprouts caused by frequent fires repeatedly top-killing small oak trees. Despite their lack of stature above ground, their root systems were extensive and could be more than 100 years old. Following even a brief cessation of fire, the oak grubs sprouted and grew vigorously, rapidly changing the renowned savannas into young forests. As the trees grew, their shade quickly reduced the prairie grasses that provided the fuel for frequent fires, further reducing fire frequency.

In addition, timber exploitation of pines (1890s) and oaks (1920s) destroyed or degraded savannas such as oak barrens and oak-pine barrens across Michigan. Those remnants that remain often lack important tree species like white pine (*Pinus strobus*) and white oak, which were selectively harvested.

In addition to changing fire frequency, immigrant settlers also introduced livestock grazing to prairie and savanna ecosystems. While grazing by native wildlife such as deer and elk occurred historically, grazing patterns of cattle and sheep were much more intensive and were often concentrated in a confined, fenced area. Grazing by livestock resulted in further reductions of grasses and forbs and, in addition to lack of fire and closed-canopy conditions, has contributed to the low floristic diversity often seen in savanna remnants today. Grazing also facilitated the introduction of nonnative weeds such as Kentucky bluegrass (*Poa pratensis*) by disturbing the soil and dispersing weed seeds through manure.

Prairies and savannas were also prone to invasion by other nonnative invasive species such as common buckthorn (*Rhamnus cathartica*) and autumn-olive (*Elaeagnus umbellata*), a problem that began in the early

OPPOSITE: Many areas formerly dominated by prairies and savannas have been converted to agriculture and other uses, leaving behind only small, fragmented pieces of habitat.

Christopher Hoving

Ryan P. O'Connor

to mid 1900s and has been accelerating ever since. Often planted for wildlife cover or landscaping in the past, the bird-dispersed fruit of these shrubs quickly found its way from planted areas into natural habitats. Many edge-loving bird species preferentially perch on large, open-grown oaks, dispersing seeds in droppings. As these plants establish, they create an easily observed spatial pattern of invasive shrubs beneath large trees in old fields. With numerous edges relative to their size, prairie and savanna remnants (often small and surrounded by fencerows, woodlots, or forests) were particularly susceptible to invasion by nonnative shrubs.

As invasive species become established, they compound negative effects on prairies and savannas. Most directly, they compete with native species and shade out native ground cover. This also reduces the prevalence of fine fuels (for example, prairie grasses) needed to carry fire, resulting in fewer fires of lower intensity. Lack of fire leads to even further declines in the diversity of native species, resulting in a complete alteration of the entire ecosystem. Invasive shrubs also affect wildlife species. Eurasian honeysuckles (*Lonicera* spp.) attract nesting songbirds, but their low branches facilitate increased predation by raccoons (*Procyon lotor*) and other pests. In some cases, impacts to wildlife have an unexpected influence on the entire ecosystem. For example, sprawling clumps of autumn-olive have been shown to harbor small mammals like voles, which in turn leads to higher seed predation of acorns and herbivory of small oak seedlings, accelerating the decline of this important tree species.

Today, many former oak savannas have almost completely closed canopies and now form many of the oak forests that presently occur in southern Lower Michigan. It is estimated that only 0.02 percent of the savanna originally found in the Midwest remains, declining from around 11–13 million acres (4–5 million hectares) to just a few hundred acres spread across a dozen states. In Michigan, the loss of savanna is most dramatic in the oak openings natural community, which has declined from an estimated 900,000 acres (360,500 hectares) to just a handful of acres, a loss of over 99.99 percent. Tiny remnants and restorable fragments likely exist, but the loss has been tremendous by every possible accounting. Another type of savanna has been lost altogether. Historically found only on mesic soils in southwest Michigan, bur oak plains have been completely converted to agricultural land, towns, and closed-canopy forest.

OPPOSITE: Important prairie grasses like big bluestem (*Andropogon gerardii*) (TOP) cannot survive beneath a dense tree canopy. BOTTOM: Prolonged grazing by livestock in confined areas has caused severe declines in many native plants.

RIGHT, TOP: Autumn-olive is an invasive shrub that tends to take over dry prairies and savannas. It can be recognized by the silvery scales that cover its leaves, stems, and red berries. BOTTOM: Invasive Eurasian honeysuckles have been linked to poor nesting success among songbirds.

Suzan L. Campbell

Suzan L. Campbell

Wildlife and Plants

Numerous animals and plants require prairies and savannas for their primary habitat. Many common as well as rare species are specially adapted to thrive in the diverse, dynamic environment. Due to the nearly complete loss of these ecosystems, however, many of these species have experienced drastic declines. Overall, prairies and savannas support a greater number of rare and declining species than any other terrestrial habitat type in Michigan. Despite comprising only 7 percent of the land area historically and less than 0.1 percent today, prairies and savannas still provide the primary habitat for over one-third of the species listed as endangered, threatened, or special concern in our state (figure 5). For a complete list of rare species associated with prairies and savannas, see appendixes 1 and 2.

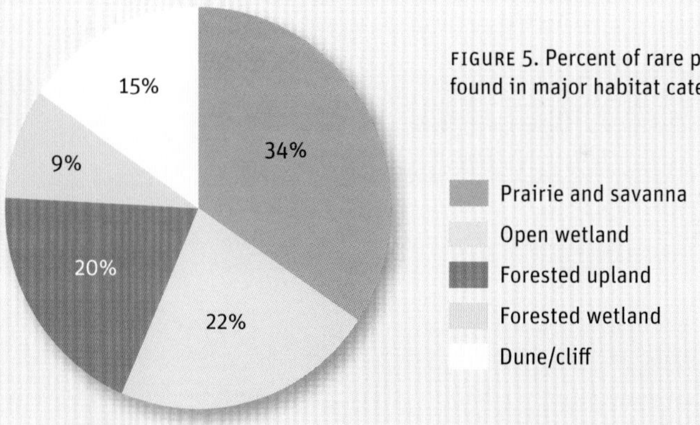

FIGURE 5. Percent of rare plants and animals found in major habitat categories.

OPPOSITE: The poweshiek skipperling (*Oarisma poweshiek*) is a rare butterfly that depends on prairie wildflowers like the black-eyed Susan (*Rudbeckia hirta*) for nectar.

Wildlife

Prairies and savannas support all types of wildlife, including birds, mammals, reptiles, and insects. Some species are generalists and will utilize any suitable grass-dominated habitat, including native prairie, planted prairie, and even old fields dominated by nonnative pasture grasses such as smooth brome (*Bromus inermis*) and timothy (*Phleum pratense*). Other species are specially adapted to specific conditions found only in high-quality natural communities.

BIRDS

Examples of birds utilizing prairies and savannas include songbirds such as grasshopper sparrow (*Ammodramus savannarum*), meadowlarks (*Sturnella* spp.), dickcissel (*Spiza americana*), and bobolink (*Dolichonyx oryzivorus*). These species can be found in many types of open grassland. The rare Henslow's sparrow (*Ammodramus henslowii*) is more restricted in its habitat needs, requiring large blocks of open land (40 acres [16 hectares] or more) with an accumulation of thick grass litter. Popular game species such as bobwhite quail (*Colinus virginianus*) are also found in prairies, along with ring-neck pheasant (*Phasianus colchicus*), introduced from Asia for hunting. Pheasants thrive where fields of robust switch grass (*Panicum virgatum*) are planted. Wild turkeys (*Meleagris gallopavo*), a species once considered in severe decline, have thrived in areas being managed for savanna. They benefit from an open canopy of large oaks, which they utilize as roosting areas. They also feed on acorns as well as insects found in adjacent openings. Management practices that maintain savannas can also benefit these and many other nongame species by increasing food availability. For example, turkeys can often be found feeding on insects in areas temporarily blackened by a prescribed burn. Over the longer term, fires can boost oak production of acorns by increasing nutrient availability and reducing competition from other trees such as red maple (*Acer*

Jerry Jourdan

Jerry Jourdan

Dave Kenyon

Dave Kenyon

CLOCKWISE FROM UPPER LEFT: Eastern meadowlark, Grasshopper sparrow, Ring-necked pheasant, Wild turkey.

LEFT: Numerous small mammals, such as the deer mouse (*Peromyscus maniculatus*), can be found in prairies and savannas.

RIGHT: Eastern fox squirrel.

rubrum), widely considered less beneficial for wildlife. Red maple has thin bark and is more susceptible to damage from fire than thick-barked oaks. As prescribed fires gradually reduce red maple, more water, nutrients, and sunlight are available for other, more beneficial tree species.

MAMMALS

The mixture of open-grown trees, dense clonal shrubs, and lush prairie vegetation provides ideal habitat for numerous mammal species. Small species like the white-footed mouse (*Peromyscus leucopus*) and prairie vole (*Microtus ochrogaster*) disperse seeds and top-kill woody plants through girdling, as they consume the lower bark of saplings. Small mammals also serve as a prey base for red fox (*Vulpes vulpes*), hawks, and owls. Squirrels thrive in savannas and play a key role in the regeneration of oak and hickory trees by caching gathered nuts. The shallow underground planting improves the odds of successful germination, and although many nuts are eaten through the winter and spring, enough remain buried to form a new crop of oak seedlings, especially in years of heavy mast, or abundant nut production.

Rabbits thrive in prairie and savanna ecosystems, especially where small patches of dense shrub cover lie in close proximity to grassy browse. Larger mammals like white-tailed deer can also be found in native grasslands and utilize savannas for birthing and raising fawns, taking advantage of the natural mixture of tree and shrub cover and lush prairie vegetation. While bats are generally not considered closely associated with savannas, recent research suggests that some species, including the federally endangered Indiana bat (*Myotis sodalis*), utilize the large, open-grown trees typically found in savannas as roosting and maternity areas. This may be due in part to increased exposure to sun and greater warmth during cool spring weather at the northern edge of the Indiana bat's range. An integral part of the ecosystem, bats provide an important service by reducing insect populations. It is estimated that a single bat consumes several thousand insects each night.

REPTILES AND AMPHIBIANS

Relatively few reptiles and amphibians are true forest species. Many prefer edge habitats, where forests grade into savannas, prairies, or wetlands. This may be due in part to a better mixture of sun and shade, allowing these cold-blooded species to more efficiently regulate their body temperature, a process called thermoregulation. In addition, a greater diversity of habitat is often associated with a greater diversity and abundance of prey species. Some species such as the eastern box turtle (*Terrapene carolina carolina*) occupy a variety of upland habitats, while others such as the spotted turtle (*Clemmys guttata*) are found primarily in high-quality wetlands, including wet prairie. One requirement all turtles have is suitable nesting areas. These include warm, open, sandy slopes and hillsides typically found in remnant savannas. As savannas

LEFT: Box turtles can live to be up to 100 years old.

RIGHT: Spotted turtles are extremely rare and require high-quality wetlands free of pollution.

OPPOSITE: Michigan is one of the last strongholds for the rare eastern massasauga rattlesnake. Ordinarily quite docile, it rarely strikes unless stepped on or picked up.

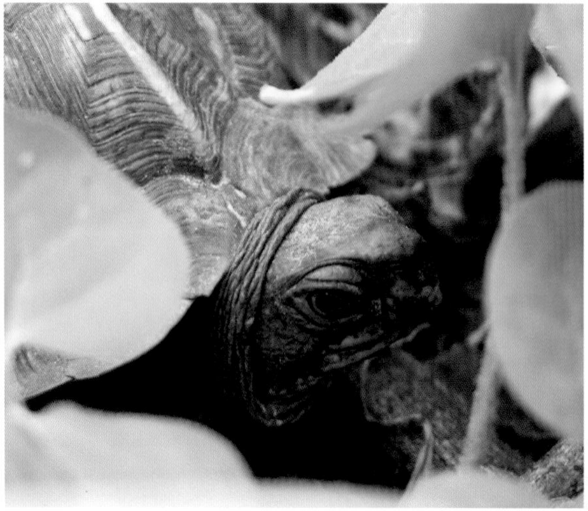

Dan Kennedy

Ryan P. O'Connor

have converted to closed-canopy forest, however, appropriate nesting habitat has declined, and females must travel longer distances in search of open sandy ground. As a result, turtles are often forced to cross roads or even nest on sandy road edges. Road kill has become a major source of female mortality. In addition, when eggs are laid, they often suffer from high predation rates from raccoons and other mammals. Although nest predation is problematic throughout the state, it is even more pronounced along roads and other travel corridors used by predators. Due to these threats, all turtles are protected by law in Michigan and should never be taken from the wild.

Various species of frogs and salamanders also thrive in the heterogeneous mixture of savanna and wetland habitats typically found in the glacial interlobate regions. The high frequency of scattered wetlands in these landscapes is particularly beneficial, since virtually all amphibians require aquatic breeding habitat

that is free of fish, which would otherwise consume eggs and larvae. The eastern tiger salamander (*Ambystoma tigrinum*) is one species especially at home in oak savannas as well as more open land including prairies and marshes.

Snakes can also be found in prairie and savanna habitats. Some, such as the blue racer (*Coluber constrictor foxii*), black rat snake (*Elaphe obsoleta obsoleta*), and eastern hog-nosed snake (*Heterodon platirhinos*), occur in a variety of semi-open habitats, often basking in sunny areas during cool spring mornings. Other species such as the Kirtland's snake (*Clonophis kirtlandii*) and eastern massasauga (*Sistrurus catenatus catenatus*) are concentrated in specific habitats like prairie fen in southern Lower Michigan. The combination of numerous abandoned crayfish burrows and a constant supply of groundwater, which does not freeze, provides an ideal site for hibernation during the cold winter months. In northern Lower Michigan, massasauga are found in close association with pine barrens, preferring landscapes with open, warm basking sites in close proximity to cedar swamps, which are utilized during hibernation. Although the massasauga is Michigan's only venomous snake, it is relatively docile and will rarely strike unless stepped on, picked up, or harassed. Having declined throughout much of its former range in the Midwest due to habitat loss and persecution, the massasauga remains locally common in Michigan, the last stronghold for this species.

BUTTERFLIES AND OTHER INVERTEBRATES

Insects comprise the largest group of prairie and savanna fauna. Many are found only in very specific habitats and are highly dependent on particular plant species. Butterflies are one of the most visible and charismatic groups, and include exceptionally rare species like the Karner blue (*Lycaeides melissa samuelis*), a small butterfly found only in oak barrens and dry prairie edges with an abundance of wild lupine (*Lupinus perennis*), its larval host plant. The Mitchell's satyr (*Neonympha mitchellii mitchellii*) is another very rare species. Currently known from fewer than 20 sites in the world, most occur in Michigan on private land, where their prairie fen habitat is threatened by invasion of nonnative shrubs such as glossy buckthorn (*Rhamnus frangula*). Common butterflies also abound in prairies and savannas, and include the Monarch (*Danaus plexippus*), Baltimore checkerspot (*Euphydryas phaeton*), eastern-tailed blue (*Everes comyntas*), fritillaries (*Speyeria* spp.), and a dazzling array of fast-flying skippers and hairstreaks. Planting butterfly gardens full of flowering prairie plants is an increasingly popular practice that not only attracts butterflies but also provides colorful displays of native wildflowers.

Other insect species such as borer moths are highly specialized, with different species dependant on a particular species of host plant. Examples include the blazing star borer (*Papaipema beeriana*), Culver's root borer (*P. sciata*), and Silphium borer (*P. silphii*), all named after their respective host plants. Many other species are much less visible, but no less unique and integral to prairie and savanna ecosystems. Invertebrates like beetles, spittlebugs, leaf hoppers, grasshoppers, katydids, crickets, and spiders are also important parts of the diversity and function of these natural communities, whether they act as microherbivores, predators helping to keep other insect pests in check, or prey for other wildlife like turtles, snakes, and birds.

Many insects are dependent on natural prairie remnants. While highly mobile species like grassland birds can move to new areas after a fire or colonize newly planted grasslands, many insects are restricted

Dan Kennedy

Dave Kenyon

Ryan P. O'Connor

Suzan L. Campbell

CLOCKWISE FROM UPPER LEFT: The Mitchell's satyr is one of the rarest butterflies in the world, a monarch butterfly sips nectar from marsh blazing star (*Liatris spicata*), a tiger swallowtail sips nectar from marsh blazing star, a great spangled fritillary sips nectar from pasture thistle (*Cirsium discolor*).

Dave Kenyon

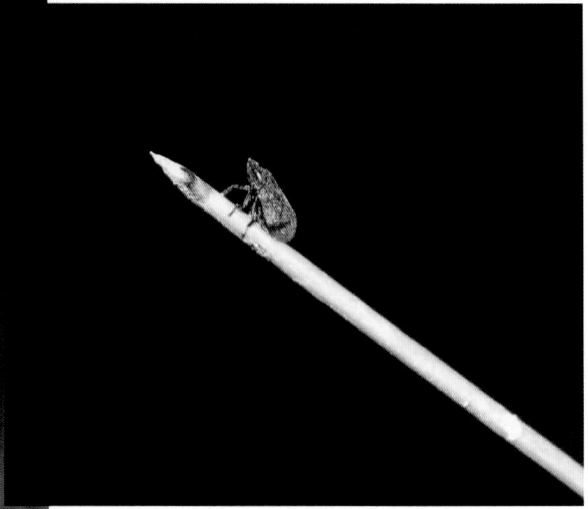

Ryan P. O'Connor

FAR LEFT: Culver's root (*Veronicastrum virginicum*) is the only host plant for the rare Culver's root borer moth.

INSET: The angular spittlebug is a tiny insect that feeds primarily on spikerush (*Eleocharis* spp.).

to tiny relict patches of habitat. Recovery from disturbances like fire may be slow. If fire consumes all available habitat or host plants, some species may even be extirpated from a site, a process made more likely by the loss of habitat and connectivity between remnant patches. Perhaps more significantly, some highly conservative remnant-dependant insects have not yet been found to colonize planted prairies, even after half a century of careful stewardship and management. For these species, an emphasis on careful restoration and management of natural, remnant prairies and savannas, rather than planted sites, is critical.

KARNER BLUE BUTTERFLY

The Karner blue is a federally threatened butterfly that is found primarily in Michigan and Wisconsin. Approximately the size of a quarter, these butterflies have a row of orange spots on the outside edge of the hind wing. Males are a colorful silvery blue on top, with females slightly duller toward the outer wing edges. Both males and females lack a threadlike tail at the base of the hind wing, a feature distinguishing the Karner blue from the more common eastern tailed blue.

Karner blue butterflies have two generations, or "flights," each summer. The first runs from mid-May through early June, and culminates in the laying of a new batch of eggs. After hatching, the larvae are tended to by ants in a mutualistic relationship in which the larvae provide a sweet secretion for the ants, and the ants in turn protect the larvae from predators and keep them free of parasites. Larvae pupate and emerge in mid-July, beginning the second flight that lasts through early August, and ends with females laying another batch of eggs that overwinter before hatching the following spring.

Karner blue larvae feed only on wild lupine, a plant that thrives in dry, partially open savannas like oak barrens. Due to the near complete loss of this habitat, however, lupine and the Karner blue are now often restricted to road edges, abandoned railroad grades, and utility rights-of-way, the only areas in many landscapes that remain partially open after decades of fire suppression and subsequent tree and shrub invasion. Often, only small remnant habitat patches and butterfly populations remain, making dispersal and interbreeding between colonies impossible. Complicating matters, the butterflies are sensitive to prescribed fire, forcing biologists to micromanage some sites in order to improve habitat without decimating butterfly populations.

Ryan P. O'Connor

ABOVE: Karner blue butterfly. RIGHT: Wild lupine is the only host plant for larvae of the Karner blue butterfly.

In other locations, however, managers are restoring larger landscapes, and the butterflies are making a comeback. At key sites in Newaygo and Muskegon counties, old pine plantations have been removed, and lupine and other barrens plants have flourished under active management. The butterflies have responded, dispersing into the newly restored habitat. Overall, biologists are making great strides in the recovery of this species by restoring oak barrens with prescribed fire, and by forming strong partnerships between government agencies, conservation organizations, and private landowners.

Charles Peirce

Plants

Throughout the seasons, the flora of prairies and savannas in Michigan is perhaps more diverse and colorful than in any other habitat in the state. From the purple violets and phloxes of spring, to the intricate orchids of summer, to the tall, waving, amber-colored grasses of fall, a tremendous array of plant species graces our prairie and savanna landscape.

Plants form the key structural and functional component of prairies. Typically, grasses and sedges make up the dominant matrix of biomass, with a diverse mix of forbs scattered throughout. In savannas, forbs can be more abundant, and oaks are also critical in providing woody structure and a partial canopy cover. With quick-drying litter containing volatile chemical compounds, oak leaves, grasses, and sedges provide much of the fine fuel needed to carry fire through the system. Likewise, both oaks and prairie grasses are characterized by extremely deep roots (6–12 feet [2–4 meters] or more) that stabilize the soil and help plants tolerate drought. The fibrous structure of grass roots allows them to soak up large amounts of rainfall, helping to increase infiltration and minimize surface runoff.

Many plants are indicators of remnant prairie and savanna habitat. These include species adapted to specific site conditions, such as birdfoot violet (*Viola pedata*) and hoary puccoon (*Lithospermum canescens*), found in drier communities such as dry sand prairie, oak barrens, and pine barrens. Other species are more general indicators, such as black-eyed Susan (*Rudbeckia hirta*), which can be found in a wide variety of both wet and dry prairies. Some plants are especially adapted to the filtered light and partially open canopy of savannas. Because virtually no high-quality remnant sites remain, determining which species are savanna specialists is difficult, but they likely include showy and distinctive plants such as lupine, Culver's root (*Veronicastrum virginicum*), woodland sunflower (*Helianthus divaricatus*), and American columbo (*Frasera caroliniensis*).

OPPOSITE: Birdfoot violet (*Viola pedata*).

Ryan P. O'Connor

Prairies and savannas are at their most colorful in late summer and fall, when blazing star (*Liatris* spp.), goldenrods (*Solidago* spp.), asters (*Aster* spp.), and prairie grasses are at their peak. Some grasses, such as big bluestem (*Andropogon gerardii*) and Indian grass (*Sorghastrum nutans*), can be found in nearly every type of prairie and savanna community throughout the state. Others, such as porcupine grass (*Stipa spartea*), are found primarily in specialized habitats like oak barrens. In this species, awns (needle-like projections attached to each seed) that resemble porcupine quills reach up to eight inches (20 centimeters) in length. The awns are hygroscopic, curling in a spiral upon drying, only to straighten again when moistened with rain. Over time, this repeated spiral curling and straightening acts to drill the seed into the soil, facilitating germination in a fascinating fashion.

In addition to their beauty and ecological function, many plants provide important benefits to wildlife. Dominant trees like bur, white, and black oak provide food in the form of acorn mast to a host of birds and mammals, including deer and turkey. The fruit of smaller trees and shrubs such as hazelnuts (*Corylus* spp.), serviceberries (*Amelanchier* spp.), hawthorns (*Crataegus* spp.), and cherries (*Prunus* spp.) is also heavily utilized, especially by birds. Wildflowers and grasses not only provide browse but also support a wide variety of insects. Many of our most showy wildflowers attract butterflies searching for nectar, including butterfly weed (*Asclepias tuberosa*), swamp milkweed (*A. incarnata*), wild bergamot (*Monarda fistulosa*), horsemint (*M. punctata*), black-eyed Susan, gray-headed coneflower (*Ratibida pinnata*),

Ryan P. O'Connor

Ryan P. O'Connor

LEFT: Rough blazing star (*Liatris aspera*).

RIGHT: Indian grass (*Sorghastrum nutans*).

Missouri ironweed (*Vernonia missurica*), coreopsis (*Coreopsis* spp.), and various asters. Goldenrods also provide nectar for butterflies and other insects. Contrary to popular belief, goldenrods are not a source of hay-fever allergies, since pollen is not released into the air but is spread directly from flower to flower by insects. More typically, allergies in summer are caused by wind-dispersed pollen from ragweed and grasses.

Some plants have highly specialized relationships with insects, serving as host plants for developing larvae. Examples include the well-known Monarch butterfly, which feeds exclusively on milkweed (*Asclepias* spp.), and the rare Karner blue butterfly, whose larvae eat only wild lupine. Other butterflies depend on lupine as a host plant as well, including the rare persius dusky wing (*Erynnis persius*) and frosted elfin (*Incisalia irus*). Additional wildflowers of prairies that serve as host plants include false foxglove (*Aureolaria* spp.), used by the Baltimore checkerspot; violets, utilized by numerous species of

OPPOSITE: Woodland sunflower (*Helianthus divaricatus*).

LEFT TO RIGHT: Swamp milkweed is often visited by butterflies like Edward's hairstreak; Horsemint (*Monarda punctata*); Stiff goldenrod (Solidago rigida); the dusted skipper (inset), a rare butterfly, requires little bluestem (far right) as a larval host plant.

Charles Peirce

Charles Peirce

fritillaries; and wild indigo (*Baptisia* spp.), which is a host for its namesake, the wild indigo dusky wing (*Erynnis baptisiae*). Trees serve as host plants as well. Hop tree (*Ptelea trifoliata*), an uncommon small tree of dry savannas, is preferred by giant swallowtail (*Papilio cresphontes*). Even grasses like little bluestem (*Schizachyrium scoparium*) and poverty grass (*Danthonia spicata*) host a myriad of species, including Leonard's skipper (*Hesperia leonardus*) and the rare ottoe skipper (*Hesperia ottoe*) and dusted skipper (*Atrytonopsis hianna*). Many of these butterflies have suffered severe declines and are listed as threatened or endangered species in the state, as their prairie and savanna habitat and host plants have dwindled from lack of management.

Low diversity of native plants is an increasing problem in both degraded remnants and planted prairies and savannas. In high-quality remnants, all but the driest prairies and savannas can contain 80 to 100 native

Ryan P. O'Connor

Brian Piccolo

species or more. Degraded remnants may have half as many species. In some planted grasslands, diversity may be limited to 10 native species or less, of which only one or two may dominate, though examples of diverse prairie plantings can be found at several parks and nature preserves.

Many natural prairie remnants are still high in diversity, but abundance has shifted over time. A lack of fire often leads to an overabundance of dominant grasses and a decline in plants of short stature, species capable of fixing nitrogen such as legumes, and small-seeded species like orchids. Invasion by trees and shrubs, as well as livestock grazing, has also led to drastic declines. Nonnative invasive species have become tremendously

Ryan P. O'Connor

Charles Peirce

problematic at many sites. In addition to competing for growing space, some, such as spotted knapweed (*Centaurea maculosa*), release allelopathic chemicals that kill or inhibit the growth of native plants.

Virtually all prairie and savanna plants are adapted to and benefit from periodic burns. Without fire, woody species encroach and litter builds up, smothering small wildflowers and preventing seeds from reaching mineral soil and germinating. Prescribed burns are increasingly being used to maintain remnant prairies and savannas, helping to ensure that these diverse parts of our natural heritage will not be lost.

LEFT: Spotted knapweed is a highly invasive species in dry, sandy habitats.

OPPOSITE, INSET: Land stewards from the Michigan Nature Association conduct a prescribed burn to restore lakeplain prairie habitat. RIGHT: The eastern prairie fringed orchid is one of the showiest and rarest plants in Michigan.

EASTERN PRAIRIE FRINGED ORCHID

The eastern prairie fringed orchid (*Platanthera leucophaea*) is one of the showiest and rarest plants in Michigan. Standing up to three feet tall, a mature individual can have more than 40 individual flowers on a single stalk, each with finely dissected, fringed lower petals. The flower emits a sweet fragrance at night that attracts hawkmoths (*Sphinx* and other species). These moths have long tongues capable of reaching nectar held deep within a long floral spur. As moths cling to the flower, perfectly positioned pollen sacs stick to their tongues and are deposited on the next flower in an elaborate pollination scheme.

Once occurring in vast stretches of open lakeplain prairie, the orchid is now largely restricted to isolated remnants along Saginaw Bay and Lake Erie. Populations number only in the hundreds, with many sites threatened by shrub invasion and altered land-use patterns. Historically, the orchid and its lakeplain prairie associates migrated inland when naturally fluctuating Great Lakes water levels rose slowly over many years, and dispersed back shoreward as lake levels fell. As the land was settled, ditches were dug, drain tiles were installed, and the rich lakeplain prairies were converted to agriculture in all but the most marginal areas. Simultaneously, natural fires that once kept prairies open were suppressed, allowing trees and shrubs to choke out the orchid and other wildflowers.

Since the mid-1900s, the natural beauty of the lakeshore has led to a housing boom along the Great Lakes coastline. More recently, nonnative aquatic plant species have invaded shorelines that remain undeveloped. One of the most problematic is an invasive subspecies of giant reed (*Phragmites australis* subsp. *australis*), a grass that can grow up to 20 feet (about 6 meters) tall and form dense monocultures hundreds of acres in size. Together, these factors have grossly altered orchid habitat both along the lakeshore and inland, effectively cutting off habitat at both ends. This

Mac Deuparo

leaves the orchid population unable to cope with changing water levels and in potential danger of severe declines. Continued low Great Lakes water levels could leave soils too dry to support the plants, but rising water may mean colonies are flooded out and overrun by a new wave of invasive species. Making matters more complicated, the moths that pollinate the orchid are found primarily in more upland prairie and savanna habitats, many of which have been eliminated or reduced to tiny remnants.

Fortunately, land managers at the Michigan Nature Association and Michigan Department of Natural Resources are working to restore lakeplain prairie communities that provide orchid habitat through shrub removal, prescribed burns, and control of invasive species. In conjunction with ongoing management, the Michigan Natural Features Inventory is simultaneously conducting research and monitoring to track the orchid's response to management activities. Future work is planned that will expand management to adjacent land owned by the state, enlarging the habitat and allowing all prairie species to thrive for future generations to enjoy.

Ryan P. O'Connor

Prairie and Savanna Classification in Michigan

Prairie or Savanna?

Ecologists characterize prairies and savannas in two primary ways, first by vegetative characters, such as the frequency and canopy coverage of trees, and second by ecological characters, such as soil moisture. In general, if a site has between 1 and 30 canopy trees (usually oak) per acre (3–74 trees per hectare), it is considered a savanna. This equates roughly with a canopy cover between 5 and 60 percent. Keeping these general guidelines in mind, it is also important to remember that prairies and savannas were often intermingled on the landscape. Never static, this balance changed over time depending on the weather and fire frequency. In prolonged periods of drought and frequent fires, prairies may have expanded, but several decades of abundant rainfall and few fires would have allowed trees to mature, returning prairies to savannas. This dynamic process of altering prairie and savanna dominance is termed a shifting landscape mosaic.

OPPOSITE: Prairies, savannas, and oak forests occur in a shifting landscape mosaic in which canopy coverage and species dominance changes over time in relation to variations in local climate and fire frequency.

TABLE 2. Prairie and Savanna Community Types Found in Michigan with Global and State Ranks

COMMUNITY	RANKING: STATE	GLOBAL
PRAIRIE		
dry sand prairie	S2	G3
dry-mesic prairie	S1	G3
hillside prairie	S1	G3
lakeplain wet prairie	S1	G2
lakeplain wet-mesic prairie	S1	G1
mesic prairie	S1	G2
mesic sand prairie	S1	G2
wet prairie	S2	G3
wet-mesic prairie	S2	G2
wet-mesic sand prairie	S2	G2G3
SAVANNA		
bur oak plains	SX	G1
lakeplain oak openings	S1	G1G2
oak barrens	S1	G3
oak openings	S1	G1
oak-pine barrens	S2	G2
pine barrens	S2	G2

NOTE: A rank of S1 or G1 designates a community as *critically imperiled* in the state or world, S2 or G2 as *imperiled*, S3 or G3 as *rare and vulnerable*. SX designates a *state-extirpated community*. Combinations such as G2G3 signify the rank is either G2 or G3, with more information needed to make a final determination.

With the combined effects of more than a century of agriculture, grazing, and fire suppression, this shifting mosaic has been radically altered, and many remnant prairies may now appear to resemble savanna or shrubland. Furthermore, remnant savanna may appear to be almost completely forested, with just a few scattered openings. There is also an issue of scale. What may appear today as a small remnant prairie surrounded by forest is often only a small opening within what was formerly a much larger savanna. Historically this was common, with many Michigan prairies occurring as relatively small openings nestled within a broader savanna landscape. It is important to recognize both the current condition (for example, closed-canopy forest) as well as the historical condition (for example, savanna) of any given site, especially in the context of land management, restoration, and conservation.

Rarity

Prairies and savannas are among the most endangered ecosystems in the nation and world. Ecologists assign state and global ranks that correspond with the rarity of species and communities, ranging from 1 to 5, with 1 being critically imperiled and 5 being common and secure from a state (S rank) or global (G rank) conservation perspective. Of the 16 prairie and savanna communities found in Michigan, all are rated G3 or rarer, with many falling into the globally endangered and threatened categories of G1 and G2 (table 2). For comparison, plants and animals with similar ratings of G1 and G2 are often legally protected and listed on the federal threatened and endangered species list.

Types of Prairie and Savanna

Prairies and savannas are often classified based on ecological characteristics such as moisture regime. The Michigan Natural Features Inventory recognizes 16 different types of prairies and savannas, which exist across a wide spectrum of moisture conditions, ranging from wet to dry (table 1). For a complete list of all Michigan communities, refer to Natural Communities of Michigan: Classification and Description, available on the Michigan Natural Features Inventory (MNFI) website. Many of the communities are more thoroughly discussed in abstracts, which are also available online. These documents provide detailed information on ecological characteristics, distribution, and flora and fauna, as well as thorough lists of references.

WET AND WET-MESIC PRAIRIES AND SAVANNAS

Examples of wet prairie communities include wet prairie, wet-mesic prairie, wet-mesic sand prairie, lakeplain wet prairie, and lakeplain wet-mesic prairie. Prairie fen shares similar vegetation with wet prairie systems, although prairie fen soils, composed primarily of finely decomposed organic matter (that is, peat), differ from the mineral soils of true prairies. Lakeplain oak openings is a type of savanna that sometimes occurs in wet swales of the glacial lakeplain. More commonly, however, the community is found on upland sandy ridges and is generally described as a dry-mesic community. By contrast, the distribution of wet and wet-mesic prairie ranges across much of the southern Lower Peninsula, with the lakeplain supporting lakeplain wet prairie, lakeplain wet-mesic prairie, and wet-mesic sand prairie, and the interlobate regions supporting wet prairie, wet-mesic prairie, wet-mesic sand prairie, and prairie fen (figure 6). All wet and wet-mesic prairie and savanna communities have water at or near the surface and are dominated by plants typically found in wetlands.

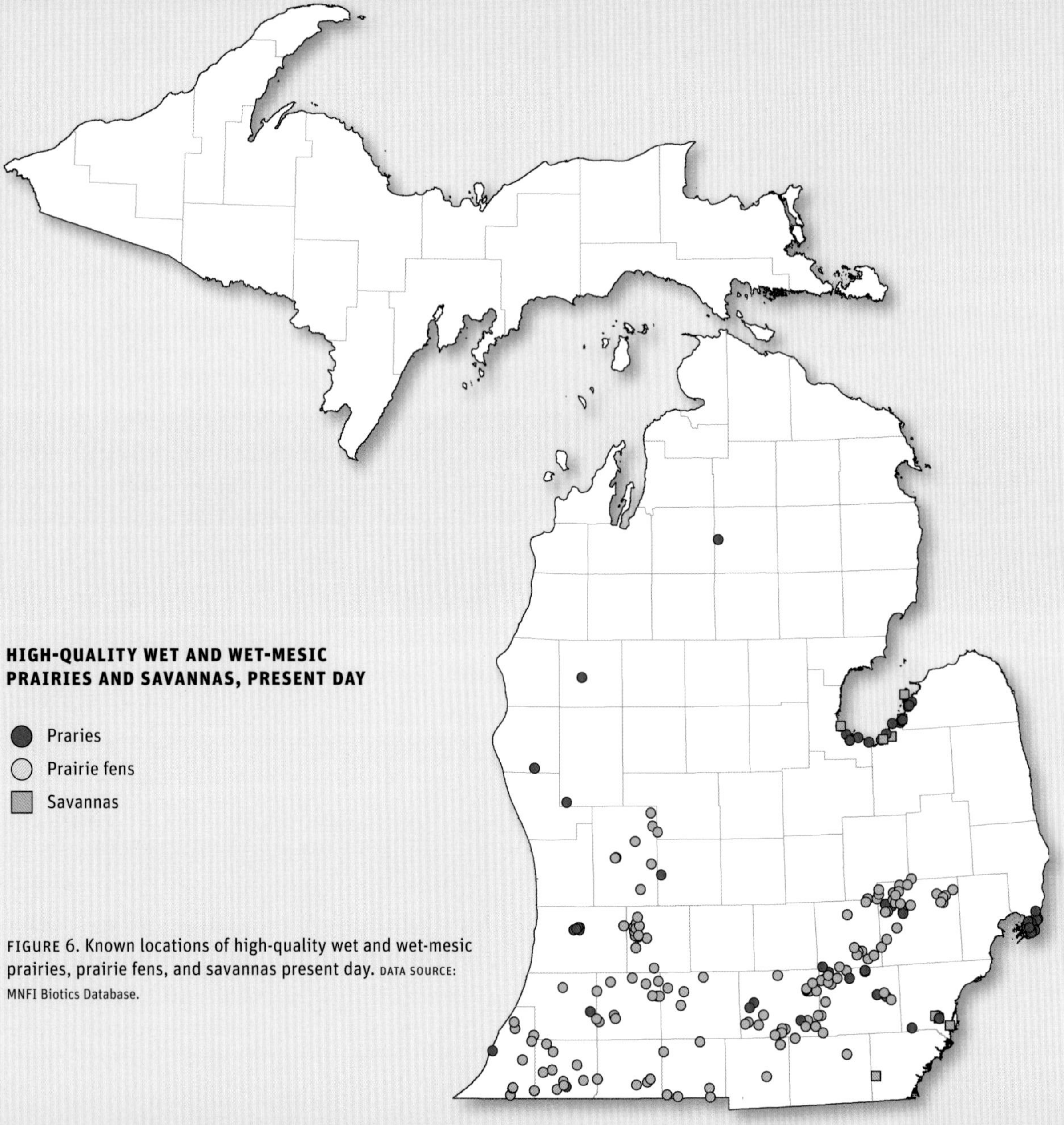

FIGURE 6. Known locations of high-quality wet and wet-mesic prairies, prairie fens, and savannas present day. DATA SOURCE: MNFI Biotics Database.

OPPOSITE: Lakeplain wet-mesic prairie in late summer.

PHYSICAL CHARACTERISTICS In general, wet prairie communities are located in glacial outwash plains along the margins of lakes, streams, and other moist depressions, as well as within glacial lakeplains near the Great Lakes, primarily near Lakes Huron and Erie. Soils of both the wet prairies and wet savannas (that is, lakeplain oak openings) are often loamy with a pH that is neutral to high (7–8), except when found in conjunction with acidic sands. Water levels fluctuate seasonally, often being as much as two feet (60 centimeters) higher in spring than in late summer. Water levels may also vary from year to year, especially at sites found on glacial lakeplains. Lakeplain prairies and oak openings and the adjacent Great Lakes are connected by a common hydrology. As Great Lakes water levels rise and fall cyclically over the years, so too does the groundwater of nearby lakeplain prairies. Other inland wetlands are also affected by the hydrologic cycles of the Great Lakes, but to a somewhat lesser degree.

ECOLOGICAL PROCESSES Hydrology is critical for maintaining wet prairies and lakeplain oak openings in an open condition. Because roots of many woody plant species have difficulty growing in saturated soils with low oxygen, trees and shrubs are often limited to slightly drier habitats. However, some species have adaptations that allow them to survive in wet conditions, including dogwood (*Cornus* spp.), willow (*Salix* spp.), tamarack (*Larix laricina*), American elm (*Ulmus americana*), bur oak, red maple, and green ash (*Fraxinus pennsylvanica*). Despite being wet, frequent surface fires occurred historically and were essential to sustaining an open habitat and high biological diversity.

CHARACTERISTIC COMMON PLANTS AND ANIMALS

Grasses and Sedges

- Big bluestem (*Andropogon gerardii*) (primarily wet-mesic sites)
- Blue-joint grass (*Calamagrostis canadensis*)
- sedges (e.g., *Carex bebbii, C. stricta, C. aquatilis*)
- Twig-rush (*Cladium mariscoides*)
- Rush (*Juncus balticus*)
- Switch grass (*Panicum virgatum*) (primarily wet-mesic sites)
- Bulrush (*Scirpus acutus*)
- Prairie cordgrass (*Spartina pectinata*)
- Indian grass (*Sorghastrum nutans*) (primarily wet-mesic sites)

Wildflowers

- Purple gerardia (*Agalinis purpurea*)
- Thimbleweed (*Anemone virginica*)
- Swamp milkweed (*Asclepias incarnata*)
- Asters (e.g., *Aster novae-angliae, A. puniceus, A. firmus, A. umbellatus*)
- Showy lady's slipper (*Cypripedium reginae*)
- Bottle gentian (*Gentiana andrewsii*)
- Fringed gentian (*Gentianopsis crinita*)
- Grass-of-Parnassus (*Parnassia glauca*)
- Mountain-mint (*Pycnanthemum virginianum*)
- Gray-headed coneflower (*Ratibida pinnata*)
- Prairie dock (*Silphium terebinthinaceum*)
- Goldenrods (e.g., *Solidago ohioensis, S. riddellii*)
- Tall meadow-rue (*Thalictrum dasycarpum*)
- Ironweed (*Vernonia* spp.)
- Culver's root (*Veronicastrum virginicum*) (primarily wet-mesic sites)
- Golden alexanders (*Zizia aurea*)

Trees and Shrubs

- Red maple (*Acer rubrum*)
- Chokeberry (*Aronia melanocarpa*)
- Red-osier dogwood (*Cornus stolonifera*)
- Silky dogwood (*C. amomum*)
- Green ash (*Fraxinus pennsylvanica*)
- Michigan holly (*Ilex verticillata*)
- Tamarack (*Larix laricina*) (primarily in prairie fens)
- Bur oak (*Quercus macrocarpa*)
- Swamp white oak (*Q. bicolor*)

- Pin oak (*Q. palustris*)
- Shrubby cinquefoil (*Potentilla fruticosa*)
- Swamp rose (*Rosa palustris*)
- Poison sumac (*Toxicodendron vernix*)

Birds

- Sandhill crane (*Grus canadensis*)
- Sedge wren (*Cistothorus platensis*)
- Common yellowthroat (*Geothlypis trichas*)
- Song sparrow (*Melospiza melodia*)
- Swamp sparrow (*M. georgiana*)
- Red-winged blackbird (*Agelaius phoeniceus*)

Reptiles and Amphibians

- Eastern newt (*Notophthalmus viridescens*)
- Western chorus frog (*Pseudacris triseriata*)
- Northern leopard frog (*Rana pipiens*)
- Pickerel frog (*R. palustris*)
- Snapping turtle (*Chelydra serpentine*)
- Painted turtle (*Chrysemys picta*)
- Northern water snake (*Nerodia sipedon sipedon*)
- Queen snake (*Regina septemvittata*)
- Butler's garter snake (*Thamnophis butleri*)
- Northern ribbon snake (*T. sauritus septentrionalis*)

Mammals

- Northern short-tailed shrew (*Blarina brevicauda*)
- Southeastern shrew (*Sorex longirostris*)
- Beaver (*Castor canadensis*)
- Meadow jumping mouse (*Zapus hudsonius*)
- Meadow vole (*Microtus pennsylvanicus*)
- Mink (*Mustela vison*)

CHARACTERISTIC RARE PLANTS AND ANIMALS

Plants

- Tall green milkweed (*Asclepias hirtella*)
- Sullivant's milkweed (*A. sullivantii*)
- Prairie Indian-plantain (*Cacalia plantaginea*)
- White lady-slipper (*Cypripedium candidum*)
- Shooting-star (*Dodecatheon meadia*)
- Queen-of-the-prairie (*Filipendula rubra*)
- Spotted phlox (*Phlox maculata*)
- Eastern prairie fringed orchid (*Platanthera leucophaea*)

- Canadian burnet (*Sanguisorba canadensis*)
- Clinton's bulrush (*Scirpus clintonii*)
- Tall nut-rush (*Scleria triglomerata*)
- Rosinweed (*Silphium integrifolium*)
- Prairie dropseed (*Sporobolus heterolepis*)
- Edible valerian (*Valeriana edulis var. ciliata*)

Birds

- American bittern (*Botaurus lentiginosus*)
- Northern harrier (*Circus cyaneus*)
- King rail (*Rallus elegans*)
- Short-eared owl (*Asio flammeus*)

Reptiles and Amphibians

- Blanchard's cricket frog (*Acris crepitans blanchardi*)
- Spotted turtle (*Clemmys guttata*)
- Blanding's turtle (*Emydoidea blandingii*)
- Kirtland's snake (*Clonophis kirtlandii*)
- Eastern fox snake (*Elaphe vulpina gloydi*) (restricted to southeastern lakeplain prairies)
- Eastern massasauga (*Sistrurus catenatus catenatus*)

Suzan L. Campbell

Lakeplain prairie and lakeplain oak openings, with prairie dock in foreground.

A

Suzan L. Campbell

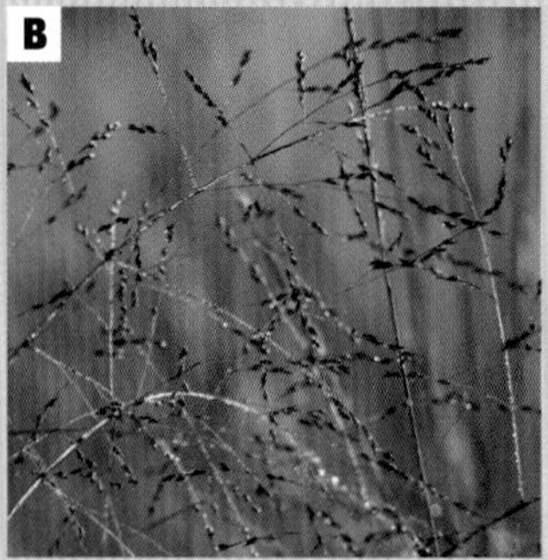

B

Dave Kenyon

C

Ryan P. O'Connor

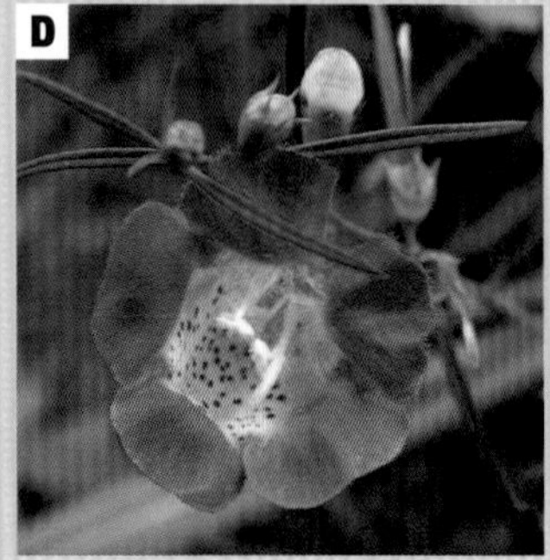

D

Suzan L. Campbell

E

Charles Peirce

F

Charles Peirce

Charles Peirce

Suzan L. Campbell

Charles Peirce

Ryan P. O'Connor

Susan R. Crispin

Charles Peirce

Susan R. Crispin

Bradford Slaughter

Michael A. Sanders

Barb Barton

COMMON SPECIES

A. Bluejoint grass (*Calamagrostis canadensis*).

B. Switch grass (*Panicum virgatum*).

C. Prairie cordgrass (*Spartina pectinata*).

D. Purple gerardia (*Agalinis purpurea*).

E. New England aster (*Aster novae-angliae*).

F. Bottle gentian (*Gentiana andrewsii*).

G. Grass-of-Parnassus (*Parnassia glauca*).

H. Gray-headed coneflower (*Ratibida pinnata*).

I. Ironweed (*Vernonia* sp.).

J. Pickerel frog.

RARE SPECIES

K. Prairie Indian-plantain (*Cacalia plantaginea*).

L. Small white lady-slipper (*Cypripedium candidum*).

M. Shooting-star (*Dodecatheon meadia*).

N. Spotted phlox (*Phlox maculata*).

O. King rail.

P. Blanding's turtle.

THE LAKEPLAIN PRAIRIES AND OAK OPENINGS OF ALGONAC STATE PARK

Robert E. Clancy

Volunteers assist with seed collection to restore lakeplain prairies at Algonac State Park.

Lakeplain prairies and oak openings are among the rarest natural communities in the state. Because they are restricted to land formerly covered by glacial precursors to the southern Great Lakes, the only places they occur in the world are along the shores of Lake Huron and Lake Erie. Once covering tens of thousands of acres, more than 99 percent of land formerly occupied by lakeplain prairie and oak openings has been lost to agriculture, development, and conversion to closed-canopy forest. Some of the largest, highest quality examples that remain in Michigan occur at Algonac State Park in St. Clair County.

The natural communities at the park are dictated by subtle yet important differences in topography and soil type. The lowest elevations are often inundated by water from the St. Clair River, which flows from Lake Huron south to Lake St. Clair. There, one can find Great Lakes marsh, a natural community dominated by cattails, tall sedges, and rushes. Inland and slightly higher in elevation, lakeplain wet prairie dominates, covered in a lush growth of grasses, sedges, and forbs. Crossing a small ridge only a foot (about 30 cm) high, the area abruptly transitions to lakeplain wet-mesic prairie, with noticeably firmer, drier soil underfoot and a greater abundance of big bluestem, Indian grass, and prairie cordgrass. This in turn grades in lakeplain oak openings, perched on the slight rise of an old beach ridge, with sparse, scattered trees on the prairie margin and a greater abundance of open-grown oaks toward the interior. Finally, the landscape transitions into a more closed-canopy forest, where the ground falls imperceptibly away into wet-mesic flatwoods, characterized by level topography and clay soils inundated with standing water in the spring, but dry in the summer.

Periodic fire and hydrology are the ecological processes that shaped these communities. Naturally fluctuating Great Lakes water levels keep open areas free of trees during periods of high water, and droughty soils and fire put strains on trees and shrubs during low water, helping to maintain an open condition. These processes have been somewhat disrupted at the park, however. A large ditch once dug to facilitate drainage disrupts natural water movement. Deprived of critical moisture, wet and wet-mesic communities are threatened with conversion to shrubs and trees. Fire suppression is also problematic, enhancing the loss of prairie and oak openings as woody plants encroach. Finally, invasive species like giant reed have taken over the Great Lakes marsh and areas near the ditch, and garlic mustard (*Alliaria petiolata*) and Eurasian honeysuckles, buckthorn, and multiflora rose (*Rosa multiflora*) have invaded former savannas.

Recently dedicated as a State Natural Area, portions of Algonac State Park are being widely recognized for their highly unique natural communities and the more than 20 rare species that occur there. The park has also received significant attention from land managers and volunteers through the Michigan DNR State Park Stewardship Unit. Prescribed burns are conducted routinely to restore prairie and oak openings. Where forests have taken over former savanna, they are being thinned of smaller trees, opening the canopy back up and allowing grasses and forbs to slowly recolonize. Invasive species like giant reed and garlic mustard are being set back through herbicides as well as prescribed burning. Finally, a large effort is under way to collect seed from native prairie plants for use in restoring other areas of the park. Managers also hope to eventually restore hydrology to facilitate naturally fluctuating water levels. Algonac State Park is open year-round and has a campground, paved and unpaved hiking trails, as well as interpretive displays explaining the unique natural heritage of the park.

PRAIRIE FEN WETLANDS OF THE GLACIATED MIDWEST

Prairie fens are among the most diverse natural communities in Michigan. Largely restricted to the glaciated Midwest, more prairie fens are found in Michigan than in any other state or province. This unique wetland community derives its name from the fact that vegetation is comprised of species typical of tallgrass prairies, such as big bluestem and Indian grass, as well as fens, such as tamarack and sedges. One of the most biologically diverse ecosystems in Michigan, it is home to more than two dozen rare plants and animals, including the Mitchell's satyr butterfly and the eastern massasauga, both globally rare species with their last strongholds in our state.

Hydrology is what makes prairie fens so unique and distinct from true wet prairies. Prairie fens occur only in sites with a constant flow of cold, calcareous groundwater. This leads to a buildup of organic soils (that is, peat), which are comprised of finely decomposed plant material. In contrast, true wet and wet-mesic prairies occur on mineral soil comprised of sand, silt, and clay. The Wildwing Fen is an example of a typical prairie fen. Located in Kensington Metropark in Oakland County, it lies just above a stream at the base of a moraine and is fed by a steady supply of groundwater, which picks up minerals such as calcium carbonate as it flows through the gravelly calcareous glacial deposits of the adjacent moraine. Often, the concentration of calcium carbonate is so high that it precipitates out of the groundwater, forming deposits of marl and rocklike formations known as tufa. Although often considered a lowland community, prairie fens are frequently located on gentle slopes due to the combination of hillside springs and peat buildup in constantly saturated soils, giving observers the unique experience of walking uphill in a wetland.

Because they are located in landscapes with hilly, gravelly soils, prairie fens were historically found adjacent to upland oak savannas. The dry upland savannas were subject to frequent surface fires, which continued across the adjacent fens. Fire suppression has severely affected both communities, allowing trees and shrubs to grow and shade out sun-loving grasses and wildflowers, eliminating habitat for wildlife. Elsewhere at Kensington, the remnants of overgrown savannas can still be seen in massive bur oak trees, some nearly 14 feet (about 4 meters) in circumference. In addition to being threatened by fire suppression, prairie fens are also highly susceptible to invasive species like glossy buckthorn and purple loosestrife (*Lythrum salicaria*).

Managers at Kensington and elsewhere are working to restore prairie fens. Through prescribed burning and cutting invading shrubs and trees, they are promoting nearly 100 species of native grasses and wildflowers found at the site, and improving habitat for some of Michigan's rarest wildlife.

Gary Reese

Dan Kennedy

TOP: Prairie fens contain vegetation typical of both fens and prairies.

INSET: Tamarack (*Larix laricina*) is frequently found in prairie fen habitats.

MESIC AND DRY-MESIC PRAIRIES AND SAVANNAS

Examples of mesic prairies and savannas in Michigan include mesic prairie (also commonly referred to as tallgrass or blacksoil prairie), mesic sand prairie, and bur oak plains, a savanna community dominated by bur oak. Drier examples of these prairies include hillside prairie, found mostly on south- to west-facing steep slopes above lakes and rivers, and dry-mesic prairie. Dry-mesic savannas include oak openings, once the most common type of savanna in the Midwest, as well as lakeplain oak openings, which occur along Great Lakes shorelines. This group of communities has declined in Michigan more than any other in the state, with only tiny remnants persisting in a handful of locations (figure 7). Bur oak plains have been completely extirpated and are no longer found in Michigan.

PHYSICAL CHARACTERISTICS In general, mesic prairie and savanna communities were located on glacial moraines, often on level to slightly rolling terrain. Dry-mesic prairies and savannas also occurred on the relatively rich, moist soils of moraines, as well as on level to slightly rolling areas of outwash plains, where soils were slightly poorer. Most types of mesic and dry-mesic prairie and savanna are characterized by soils of loam to sandy loam with a slightly acid to circumneutral pH (5.8–7.3). Neither too wet nor too dry, these communities readily supported numerous trees and shrubs along with a dazzling array of grasses and wildflowers.

ECOLOGICAL PROCESSES Because mesic and dry-mesic soils are ideal for tree growth, frequent fire is necessary to maintain open conditions. Historically, a heavy annual growth of grasses provided the fine fuels necessary to sustain fire, which often occurred annually. Periods of time without fire allowed trees and shrubs to rapidly establish, and open areas could be completely transformed into shrubland and forest in as little as 20 years. Because they were relatively free of trees but had fertile soils, mesic and dry-mesic prairies

HIGH-QUALITY MESIC AND DRY-MESIC PRAIRIES AND SAVANNAS, PRESENT DAY

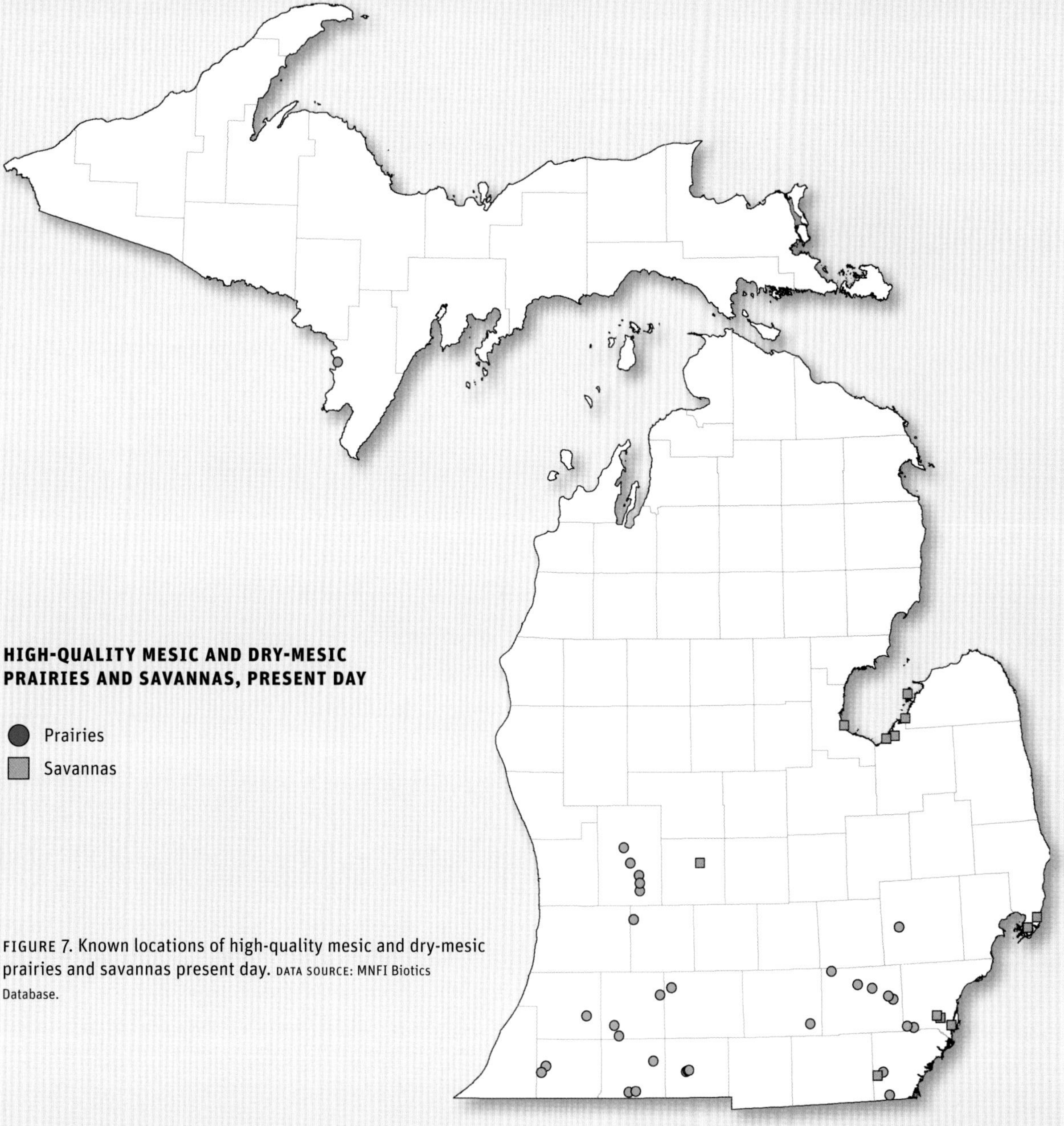

FIGURE 7. Known locations of high-quality mesic and dry-mesic prairies and savannas present day. DATA SOURCE: MNFI Biotics Database.

Bradfordd Slaughter

were among the first areas converted to agriculture. Nearby savannas made ideal sites for towns, and old savanna remnants can still be seen on some college campuses and in cemeteries. In the early 1800s, prior to the use of zip codes, some settlements were known simply by the name of the prairie they occupied, including Prairie Ronde in southwest Kalamazoo County. Once one of the largest prairies in the state, it has all but vanished, although the local township still bears its name.

CHARACTERISTIC COMMON PLANTS AND ANIMALS

Grasses and Sedges

- Big bluestem (*Andropogon gerardii*)
- Little bluestem (*Schizachyrium scoparium*)
- Indian grass (*Sorghastrum nutans*)
- Porcupine grass (*Stipa spartea*)

Wildflowers

- Yarrow (*Achillea millefolium*)
- Thimbleweed (*Anemone cylindrica*)
- Wild columbine (*Aquilegia canadensis*)
- Butterfly weed (*Asclepias tuberosa*)
- Asters (e.g., *Aster oolentangiensis, A. laevis, A. pilosus*)
- Pale Indian-plantain (*Cacalia atriplicifolia*)

- Tall coreopsis (*Coreopsis tripteris*)
- American columbo (*Frasera caroliniensis*)
- Bastard toadflax (*Comandra umbellata*)
- Tick-trefoils (e.g., *Desmodium canadense, D. illinoense, D. marilandicum*)
- Fleabanes (*Erigeron annuus, E. strigosus*)
- Flowering spurge (*Euphorbia corollata*)
- Wild strawberry (*Fragaria virginiana*)
- Veiny pea (*Lathyrus venosus*)
- Round-headed bush-clover (*Lespedeza capitata*)
- Wood lily (*Lilium philadelphicum*)
- Wild bergamot (*Monarda fistulosa*)
- Prairie phlox (*Phlox pilosa*)
- Early buttercup (*Ranunculus fascicularis*)
- Black-eyed Susan (*Rudbeckia hirta*)
- False spikenard (*Smilacina racemosa*)
- Goldenrods (e.g., *Solidago juncea, S. rigida*)
- Yellow pimpernel (*Taenidia integerrima*)
- Common spiderwort (*Tradescantia ohiensis*)

Trees and Shrubs

- Serviceberry (*Amelanchier* spp.)
- Hickories (*Carya glabra, C. ovata*)
- New Jersey tea (*Ceanothus americanus*)
- Gray dogwood (*Cornus foemina*)
- Hazelnut (*Corylus americana*)
- Hawthorn (*Crataegus crus-gallii*, etc.)
- Wild plum (*Prunus americana*)
- Hop tree (*Ptelea trifoliata*) (primarily dry-mesic sites)
- White oak (*Quercus alba*)
- Bur oak (*Q. macrocarpa*)
- Black oak (*Q. velutina*)
- Smooth sumac (*Rhus glabra*)
- Prairie rose (*Rosa carolina*)

Birds

- Wild turkey (*Meleagris gallopavo*)
- Bobwhite (*Colinus virginianus*)
- Eastern kingbird (*Tyrannus tyrannus*)
- Eastern bluebird (*Sialia sialis*)
- Indigo bunting (*Passerina cyanea*)
- Savanna sparrow (*Passerculus sandwichensis*)

OPPOSITE: Only tiny, fragmented remnants of mesic prairies exist in Michigan today.

- Bobolink (*Dolichonyx oryzivorus*)
- Eastern meadowlark (*Sturnella magna*)
- Baltimore oriole (*Icterus galbula*)

Reptiles and Amphibians

- Eastern tiger salamander (*Ambystoma tigrinum*)
- Eastern garter snake (*Thamnophis sirtalis*)
- Smooth green snake (*Opheodrys vernalis*)
- Blue racer (*Coluber constrictor foxii*)
- Eastern milk snake (*Lampropeltis triangulum triangulum*)

Mammals

- Red bat (*Lasiurus borealis*)
- Eastern cottontail (*Sylvilagus floridanus*)
- Woodchuck (*Marmota monax*)
- Thirteen-lined ground squirrel (*Spermophilus tridecemlineatus*)
- Eastern fox squirrel (*Sciurus niger*)
- Prairie deer mouse (*Peromyscus maniculatus bairdii*)
- Red fox (*Vulpes vulpes*)
- Least weasel (*Mustela nivalis*)
- White-tailed deer (*Odocoileus virginianus*)

CHARACTERISTIC RARE PLANTS AND ANIMALS

Plants

- Lead plant (*Amorpha canescens*)
- Purple milkweed (*Asclepias purpurascens*)
- Prairie false indigo (*Baptisia lactea*)
- Kitten-tails (*Besseya bullii*)
- Side-oats grama grass (*Bouteloua curtipendula*)
- Prairie coreopsis (*Coreopsis palmata*)
- Yellow fumewort (*Corydalis flavula*)
- Rattlesnake-master (*Eryngium yuccifolium*)
- White gentian (*Gentiana flavida*)
- Purple twayblade (*Liparis liliifolia*)
- Violet wood-sorrel (*Oxalis violacea*)
- Leiberg's panic-grass (*Panicum leibergii*)
- Prairie buttercup (*Ranunculus rhomboideus*)
- Hairy ruellia (*Ruellia humilis*)
- Fire pink (*Silene virginica*)
- Compass-plant (*Silphium laciniatum*)
- Eared false foxglove (*Tomanthera auriculata*)
- Prairie birdfoot violet (*Viola pedatifida*)
- Prairie golden alexanders (*Zizia aptera*)

Birds

- Barn owl (*Tyto alba*)
- Short-eared owl (*Asio flammeus*)
- Dickcissel (*Spiza americana*)
- Grasshopper sparrow (*Ammodramus savannarum*)
- Henslow's sparrow (*A. henslowii*)
- Western meadowlark (*Sturnella neglecta*)

Reptiles and Amphibians

- Eastern box turtle (*Terrapene carolina carolina*)
- Black rat snake (*Elaphe obsoleta obsoleta*)
- Eastern massasauga (*Sistrurus catenatus catenatus*)

Mammals

- Least shrew (*Cryptotis parva*)
- Indiana bat (*Myotis sodalis*)
- Prairie vole (*Microtus ochrogaster*)
- Woodland vole (*M. pinetorum*)

Dry-mesic prairie remnants are rare in Michigan.

Bradford Slaughter

A

Bradford Slaughter

B

Charles Peirce

C

Suzan L. Campbell

D

Bradford Slaughter

E

Suzan L. Campbell

F

Bradford Slaughter

Charles Peirce

Charles Peirce

Bradford Slaughter

Jerry Jourdan

Dave Kenyon

Bradford Slaughter

Bradford Slaughter

Bradford Slaughter

Charles Peirce

Bradford Slaughter

Dave Kenyon

COMMON SPECIES

A. Wild columbine (*Aquilegia canadensis*).

B. Showy tick-trefoil (*Desmodium canadense*).

C. Flowering spurge (*Euphorbia corollata*).

D. Veiny pea (*Lathyrus venosus*).

E. Round-headed bush-clover (*Lespedeza capitata*).

F. Wood lily (*Lilium philadelphicum*).

G. Wild bergamot (*Monarda fistulosa*).

H. Common spiderwort (*Tradescantia ohiensis*).

I. Prairie rose (*Rosa carolina*).

J. Savanna sparrow.

K. Woodchuck or groundhog.

RARE SPECIES

L. Leadplant (*Amorpha canescens*).

M. Prairie coreopsis (*Coreopsis palmata*).

N. Rattlesnake-master (*Eryngium yuccifolium*).

O. Fire pink (*Silene virginica*).

P. Compass-plant (*Silphium laciniatum*).

Q. Barn owl.

Bradford Slaughter

PRAIRIE RONDE AND THE OAK OPENINGS OF KALAMAZOO COUNTY

> The prairie . . . seemed wondrously beautiful and grand. It was simply in a state of nature, covered with a pretty, rank growth of grass, then dry and sere, no tree except the Big Island grove.
>
> —E. Lakin Brown, describing Prairie Ronde on November 6, 1831

Charles Peirce

Prairie Ronde, located in southwest Kalamazoo County, was once the largest mesic prairie in Michigan. Stretching over 12,000 acres (nearly 5,000 hectares), the prairie was just a small piece of a vast landscape of intermixed mesic prairie, oak openings, and oak barrens occupying well over 300 square miles (about 800 square kilometers) in present-day Kalamazoo County. Within ten years of the Treaty of Chicago in 1821, which consolidated Native American lands and opened up the area to immigrant settlers, all eight of the major prairies in the region were settled.

One of the area's earliest European settlers was thought to be the inspiration for the main character in a novel written by James Fenimore Cooper entitled *The Oak Opening*. Set in Michigan, the book's title captured what early settlers already knew: the southern portion of the state was not a dense, unbroken forest but a scenic mosaic of scattered oaks, prairie grasses, and wildflowers. An early settler described a colorful Prairie Ronde after a fire: "in a few days came the beautiful flowers, covering the whole prairie with one uniform kind and color; first the blue violet [*Viola pedatifida*]; then the purple phlox [*Phlox pilosa*], and this succeeded by some other color. In July and August, a tall, yellow flower, the name of which I do not know [possibly gray-headed coneflower (*Ratibida pinnata*) or prairie dock (*Silphium terebinthinaceum*)], mixed profusely with the tall grass, gave yellow as the predominating color " (Brown 1881, cited in Chapman 1984).

Currently, only three isolated remnants of mesic prairie remain, and the violet described as covering the ground is threatened with extirpation from the state. The oak openings that provided the setting for Cooper's book have declined from nearly a million acres (about 400,000 hectares) in circa 1800 to only a handful today. Tiny, tattered pieces of these lost landscapes can still be found in the unmowed portions of old cemeteries, on open hillsides, and along railroad tracks, which were formerly maintained by fires sparked from passing trains. Some prairie sites are being preserved and managed by land conservancies, but there are many more on both private and public land that would benefit from restoration. Time will tell if these native landscapes will be lost forever or if they will be restored to a semblance of the natural beauty described by early explorers and settlers.

LEFT: Only tiny fragments of mesic and dry-mesic prairies and savannas remain in Michigan in places such as old cemeteries and along railroads.

INSET: Purple phlox (*Phlox pilosa*).

DRY PRAIRIES AND SAVANNAS

Dry prairies and savannas are concentrated in the northern and western portions of the Lower Peninsula (figure 8). Examples include dry sand prairie, oak barrens, and oak-pine barrens, especially common in Allegan and Newaygo counties, as well as pine barrens in northern Michigan centered around Crawford County. Other small pockets of oak-pine barrens and pine barrens exist in the Upper Peninsula. Historically, oak barrens were found throughout much of the interlobate region in southern Lower Michigan as well, although most have been lost to fire suppression and now exist as closed-canopy remnants. Relative to more mesic ecosystems, a much higher proportion of dry prairies and barrens remain intact, largely due to exceptionally dry, nutrient-poor soils that made the areas unproductive for agriculture and slowed the invasion of trees and shrubs.

PHYSICAL CHARACTERISTICS Dry prairie and savanna communities are located primarily on level to rolling glacial outwash deposits of excessively drained sand and loamy sand. With an acidic pH (4.5–6.5) and dry, infertile soils, these communities exhibit sparse vegetation. This earned them the moniker "barrens" among early surveyors, a term used today to refer collectively to dry savannas. Because their sandy soils have very low water-holding capacity and low nutrient availability, dry prairies and savannas were poorly suited for agriculture. After failed attempts at farming, many landowners defaulted on tax payments and areas reverted to public ownership. As a result, many dry prairie and savanna remnants are concentrated on state and federal land.

ECOLOGICAL PROCESSES Like other types of prairies and savannas, dry prairies and barrens experienced frequent low-intensity surface fires. Pine barrens are an exception, however, being prone to more infrequent, catastrophic wildfires. In general, dry prairies and savannas likely burned less often than their

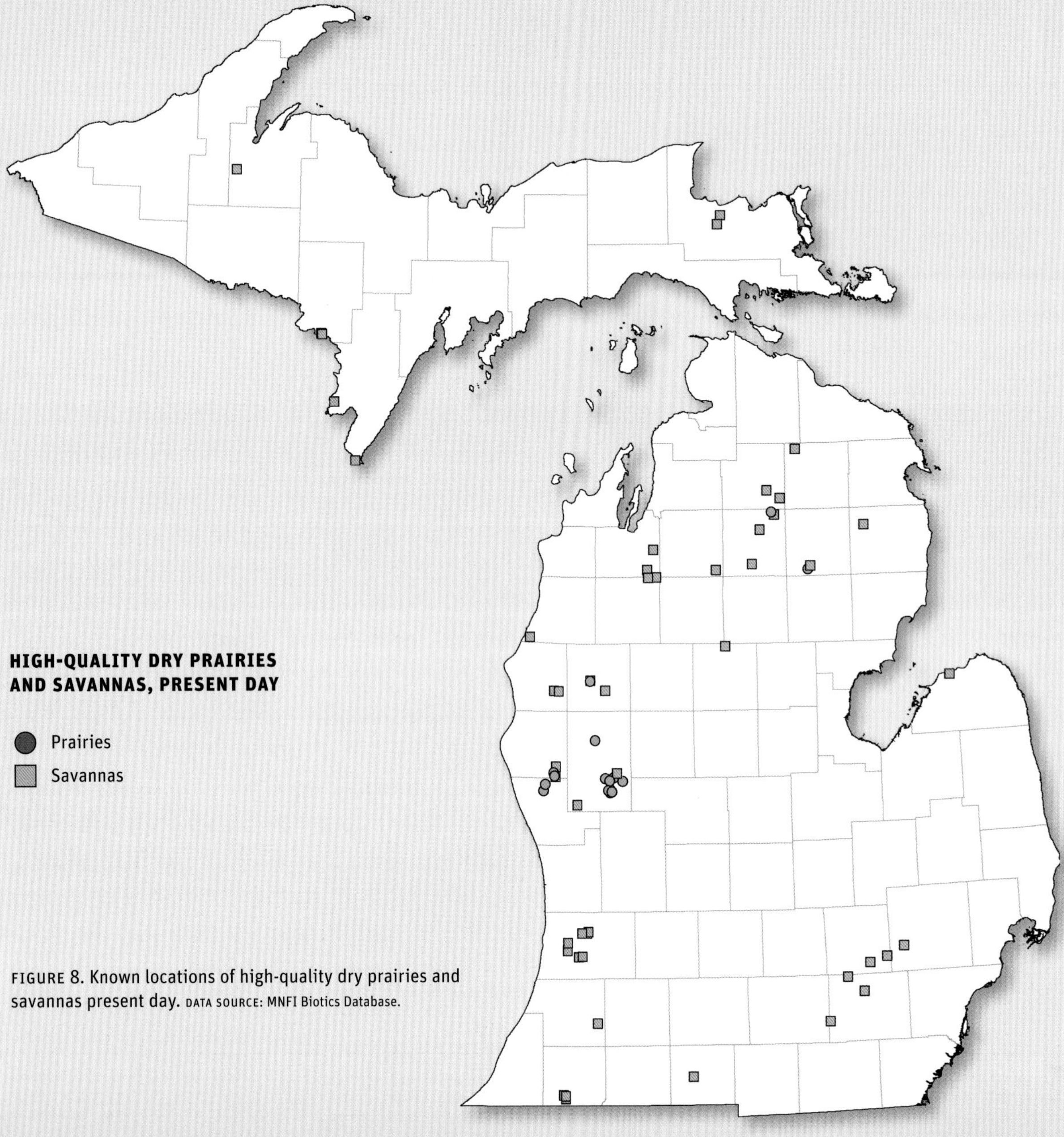

FIGURE 8. Known locations of high-quality dry prairies and savannas present day. DATA SOURCE: MNFI Biotics Database.

OPPOSITE: Wild lupine carpets the ground after a fire in an oak barrens.

more mesic counterparts. Extremely dry soil conditions and low nutrient availability slow the growth of plants and limit buildup of fine fuels needed to carry a fire. Droughty soils also restrict tree growth, which helps to maintain a relatively open condition in the modern era of fire suppression. Additionally, in the pine and oak-pine barrens of northern Michigan, open, treeless depressions act as cold air sinks. In these frost pockets, open conditions are maintained by frequent growing-season frosts, which prevent all but the hardiest trees and shrubs from establishing. Finally, historical logging of white pine and red pine (*Pinus resinosa*) has severely affected oak-pine and pine barrens, removing the important supercanopy structure. Many of these ecosystems have been slow to recover from logging, especially where seed sources to regenerate these species are lacking.

CHARACTERISTIC PLANTS AND ANIMALS

Grasses and Sedges

- Little bluestem (*Schizachyrium scoparium*)
- Three-awned grass (*Aristida purpurascens*)
- Pennsylvania sedge (*Carex pensylvanica*)
- Slender sand sedge (*Cyperus filiculmis*)
- Poverty grass (*Danthonia spicata*)
- Hair grass (*Deschampsia flexuosa*)
- June grass (*Koeleria macrantha*)
- Porcupine grass (*Stipa spartea*)

Wildflowers

- Spreading dogbane (*Apocynum androsaemifolium*)
- Butterfly weed (*Asclepias tuberosa*)
- Asters (e.g., *Aster oolentangiensis, A. ericoides*)
- Pasture thistle (*Cirsium discolor*)
- Bastard toadflax (*Comandra umbellata*)
- Sand coreopsis (*Coreopsis lanceolata*)
- Flowering spurge (*Euphorbia corollata*)
- Hairy bedstraw (*Galium pilosum*)
- Old field balsam (*Gnaphalium obtusifolium*)
- Long-bearded hawkweed (*Hieracium longipilum*)

- Common rockrose (*Helianthemum canadense*)
- Sunflowers (e.g., *Helianthus divaricatus, H. occidentalis*)
- Dwarf dandelion (*Krigia virginica*)
- Hairy bush-clover (*Lespedeza hirta*)
- Blazing stars (e.g., *Liatris aspera, L. cylindracea, L. scariosa*)
- Hoary puccoon (*Lithospermum canescens*)
- Hairy puccoon (*L. caroliniense*)
- Wild lupine (*Lupinus perennis*)
- Four-leaved loosestrife (*Lysimachia quadrifolia*)
- Horsemint (*Monarda punctata*)
- Eastern prickly-pear (*Opuntia humifusa*)
- Hairy beardtongue (*Penstemon hirsutus*)
- Racemed milkwort (*Polygala polygama*)
- Prairie cinquefoil (*Potentilla arguta*)
- Prairie ragwort (*Senecio plattensis*)
- Goldenrods (e.g., *Solidago rigida, S. nemoralis, S. speciosa, S. hispida*)
- Goat's-rue (*Tephrosia virginiana*)
- Birdfoot violet (*Viola pedata*)

Trees and Shrubs

- Serviceberries (*Amelanchier* spp.)
- Bearberry (*Arctostaphylos uva-ursi*)
- New Jersey tea (*Ceanothus americanus*)
- Sweet-fern (*Comptonia peregrina*)
- Hazelnuts (*Corylus americana, C. cornuta*)
- Hawthorns (*Crataegus* spp.)
- Jack pine (*Pinus banksiana*)
- Red pine (*P. resinosa*)
- White pine (*P. strobus*)
- Quaking aspen (*Populus tremuloides*)
- Sand cherry (*Prunus pumila*)
- Hop tree (*Ptelea trifoliata*)
- White oak (*Quercus alba*)
- Northern pin oak (*Q. ellipsoidalis*)
- Black oak (*Q. velutina*)
- Northern dewberry (*Rubus flagellaris*)
- Prairie willow (*Salix humilis*)
- Blueberries (*Vaccinium angustifolium, V. myrtilloides*)

Birds

- Field sparrow (*Spizella pusilla*)
- Vesper sparrow (*Pooecetes gramineus*)
- Lark sparrow (*Chondestes grammacus*)
- Song sparrow (*Melospiza melodia*)
- Eastern meadowlark (*Sturnella magna*)
- Brewer's blackbird (*Euphagus cyanocephalus*)
- American goldfinch (*Carduelis tristis*)

Reptiles and Amphibians

- Fowler's toad (*Bufo fowleri*)
- Smooth green snake (*Opheodrys vernalis*)
- Blue racer (*Coluber constrictor foxii*)
- Eastern hog-nosed snake (*Heterodon platirhinos*)

Mammals

- Woodchuck (*Marmota monax*)
- Thirteen-lined ground squirrel (*Spermophilus tridecemlineatus*)
- Eastern fox squirrel (*Sciurus niger*)
- Red fox (*Vulpes vulpes*)
- Badger (*Taxidea taxus*)
- Elk (*Cervus canadensis*) (restricted to northern Lower Michigan)
- White-tailed deer (*Odocoileus virginianus*)

RARE PLANTS AND ANIMALS

Plants

- Pale agoseris (*Agoseris glauca*) (restricted to northern Lower Michigan)
- Leadplant (*Amorpha canescens*)
- Dwarf milkweed (*Asclepias ovalifolia*)
- Canadian milk-vetch (*Astragalus canadensis*)
- Cooper's milk-vetch (*A. neglectus*)
- Cream wild indigo (*Baptisia leucophaea*)
- Hill's thistle (*Cirsium hillii*)
- Rough fescue (*Festuca scabrella*) (restricted to northern Lower Michigan)
- Prairie-smoke (*Geum triflorum*)
- False boneset (*Kuhnia eupatorioides*)
- Furrowed flax (*Linum sulcatum*)
- Pale beardtongue (*Penstemon pallidus*)
- Cleft phlox (*Phlox bifida*)
- Alleghany plum (*Prunus alleghaniensis var. davisii*)

- White goldenrod (*Solidago bicolor*)
- Virginia spiderwort (*Tradescantia virginiana*)
- Bastard pennyroyal (*Trichostema dichotomum*)

Birds

- Kirtland's warbler (*Dendroica kirtlandii*) (restricted to northern Lower Michigan and Upper Peninsula)
- Prairie warbler (*D. discolor*)
- Grasshopper sparrow (*Ammodramus savannarum*)

Reptiles and Amphibians

- Eastern box turtle (*Terrapene carolina carolina*)
- Eastern massasauga (*Sistrurus catenatus catenatus*)

Mammals

- Least shrew (*Cryptotis parva*)

Michael A. Kost

Wild lupine carpets the ground after a fire in an oak barrens.

Suzan L. Campbell

Ryan P. O'Connor

Charles Peirce

Ryan P. O'Connor

Dan Kennedy

Charles Peirce

Christopher Hoving

Charles Peirce

Suzan L. Campbell

Charles Peirce

Jerry Jourdan

Bradford Slaughter

Bradford Slaughter

Charles Peirce

Dan Kennedy

COMMON SPECIES

A. Spreading dogbane (*Apocynum androsaemifolium*).

B. Prairie heart-leaved aster (*Aster oolentangiensis*).

C. Sand coreopsis (*Coreopsis lanceolata*).

D. Western sunflower (*Helianthus occidentalis*).

E. A silver-spotted skipper sips nectar from northern blazing star (*Liatris scariosa*).

F. Hairy puccoon (*Lithospermum caroliniense*).

G. Four-leaved loosestrife (*Lysimachia quadrifolia*).

H. Eastern prickly-pear (*Opuntia humifusa*).

I. Hairy beardtongue (*Penstemon hirsutus*).

J. Goat's-rue (*Tephrosia virginiana*).

K. Eastern meadowlark.

RARE SPECIES

L. Pale agoseris (*Agoseris glauca*).

M. Hill's thistle (*Cirsium hillii*).

N. Prairie-smoke (*Geum triflorum*).

O. Eastern massasauga rattlesnake.

David L. Cuthrell

Dave Kenyon

PINE BARRENS AND THE KIRTLAND'S WARBLER

A native savanna community, pine barrens are located in northern Lower Michigan and in parts of the Upper Peninsula. They are found on flat to rolling terrain with acidic, low-nutrient, sandy soil. Despite their barren look, they are not wastelands, but instead are highly specialized grass-dominated ecosystems that provide important wildlife habitat to a variety of animals, including many game species. In particular, the soft, dense grasses and sedges provide excellent grazing and fawning areas for white-tailed deer, while wild turkeys thrive on the acorns produced by groves of oaks.

Pine barrens also contain more globally rare species than any other habitat in northern Michigan. Species like the Kirtland's warbler (*Dendroica kirtlandii*) can be found in the pine barrens region, nesting exclusively in young jack pine forest interspersed with scattered openings. Michigan provides breeding habitat to over 99 percent of the world's population of this exceptionally rare songbird. It is often referred to as the phoenix of the barrens because it only utilizes dense stands of jack pine and shrubs that regenerate after wildfire. To limit the risk of dangerous fires, managers now establish large plantations of jack pine for the warbler. When the species has moved on to younger growth, the trees are harvested for pulpwood, which removes fuel and reduces the risk of wildfires.

At several pine barrens in Alcona, Crawford, and Montmorency counties, private landowners are partnering with state wildlife biologists to utilize prescribed fire as a tool for maintaining habitat for other species associated with pine barrens, such as the dusted skipper butterfly and eastern massasauga rattlesnake. By conducting prescribed burns only when weather conditions meet certain criteria (avoiding high wind and very low humidity), professional fire crews can harness the benefits of fire, such as promoting grasses and wildflowers, reducing invading trees and shrubs, and encouraging natural jack pine regeneration. At the same time, prescribed burns reduce fuel loads, minimizing the risk of future catastrophic wildfires.

However, pine barrens are still prone to catastrophic wildfires today, despite efforts to prevent them. Risk is greatest in spring when warm sunny days and southerly or westerly winds rapidly dry out fine fuels. Wildfires can be minimized by being vigilant about not discarding lit cigarette butts and carefully tending campfires and burn barrels. In addition, educational efforts urge owners of houses and cabins to create "defensible space" by landscaping with plants that are less likely to catch fire, minimizing damage or loss in the event that a wildfire does occur.

LEFT: A dusted skipper sips nectar from prairie ragwort in a pine barrens.

INSET: The rare Kirtland's warbler nests only in young jack pine stands found in the pine barrens region.

Threats and Conservation

Threats

HABITAT LOSS

Over 99 percent of prairies and savannas have been lost over the past 200 years. Much of that loss can be attributed to conversion to agriculture or other development. The fertile soils and lack of trees made many of these natural communities ideal for early settlement and farming. The mass production of the steel plow made it possible to cut deep furrows through the thick prairie sod and allowed millions of acres of prairie to be settled and farmed throughout the Midwest. In addition, ditching and the installation of drain tiles converted many wet prairies to land suitable for agriculture.

More recently, habitat has been lost to rapidly expanding development as demand for suburban and rural property has increased. Oakland County, named for its historic, stately oak openings, is now one of the wealthiest counties in the state and experienced the largest population increase in the state between 1990 and 2000. As development pressure continues to increase, remnant savannas are converted to housing developments. Even wetlands, many of which are protected from development, are threatened by alterations to hydrology and an increased use of groundwater for commercial and domestic use.

Savannas have also been dramatically altered by logging. In oak barrens, a preference for white oak lumber has led to a decline in that species and a disproportionate increase in black oak. This affects more than just tree composition, since many wildlife species greatly prefer the lower tannin acorns of white oak, rather than the bitter, high-tannin acorns of black oak. Within pine barrens and oak-pine barrens, logging of white pine and, to a lesser degree, red pine has resulted in the simplification of the canopy structure and a depletion of the available red and white pine seed source.

ALTERED ECOLOGICAL PROCESSES

The alteration of ecological processes is one of the primary reasons prairies and savannas are so rare today relative to their historical extent. Processes like fire and hydrology have maintained prairies and savannas for thousands of years. When these processes are altered, the environmental conditions change, providing a competitive advantage to a different suite of species. Over time, this can lead to a wholesale change in the entire community, replacing prairie or savanna with shrubland or forest.

LACK OF FIRE More than any other altered natural process, the reduction of fire has had the greatest impact on the vegetative composition in historic prairies and savannas. Since circa 1800, the historical fire cycle has been drastically alerted, greatly reducing both the incidence and extent of fire across the landscape. Where fires once swept over several contiguous miles of prairies, savannas, and oak forest, today roads and plowed fields, along with fire suppression activities, effectively contain their spread, especially in southern Lower Michigan. In mesic and dry-mesic sites, frequent surface fires were the primary factor preventing tree and shrub invasion. Repeated fires stimulated the growth of grasses and wildflowers, and top-killed

OPPOSITE: Large open grown oaks surrounded by younger trees may indicate that a forest is actually a remnant savanna.

trees and shrubs. When fires ceased, these woody species responded vigorously, shading out sun-loving prairie plants. Often this conversion took place in as little as 20 years, although on drier or wetter sites succession might have proceeded more slowly. As trees grew, formerly open sites disappeared, converting to closed-canopy oak forests instead. Frequently, these altered natural communities can be identified today by "wolf trees," large oaks with spreading branches that grew a hundred years ago or more when sites were much more open.

A lack of fire is also problematic to wildlife requiring open habitat. In both upland and wetland natural communities, available open habitat has slowly shrunk, confining species to ever smaller habitat patches. Over time, this process has fragmented formerly large populations into genetically isolated subgroups, depriving species of critical gene flow necessary to prevent inbreeding and local extinctions.

ALTERED HYDROLOGY For more than a century, wetlands have been tiled, ditched, and filled in an attempt to make them more suitable to agriculture and development. At other sites, overuse of groundwater is suspected of lowering the water table in adjacent groundwater-fed prairie fens. Alteration of hydrology affects plant growth and composition both directly and indirectly. Often, even a slight lowering of the water table allows trees and shrubs to gain a foothold. Sites with disturbed hydrology are also more susceptible to invasion by nonnative species like glossy buckthorn, narrow-leaf cattail (*Typha angustifolia*), and giant reed. As trees and shrubs begin to dominate, their greater leaf surface-area also transpires and translocates more water than do herbaceous plants. This creates a feedback loop that further lowers the water table, gives woody species a competitive advantage, and promotes canopy closure.

In some communities such as lakeplain prairies and lakeplain oak openings, the water levels fluctuate naturally with changes in the levels of the adjacent Great Lakes. Periodic high- and low-water cycles prevent prolonged dominance by any species assemblage, and help create an exceptionally diverse

Suzan L. Campbell

Michigan Sea Grant

Glossy buckthorn (*Rhamnus frangula*) (LEFT) and giant reed (*Phragmites australis*) (RIGHT) are problematic invasive species in wetland communities.

ecosystem. Similarly, in mesic and wet-mesic sand prairies, seasonal water-level fluctuations are the norm, with high water in the spring followed by a drop in water levels and seasonal drought in late summer. Protecting the natural hydrologic processes that maintain species diversity and open conditions of these communities is a crucial component of any long-term conservation strategy.

INVASIVE SPECIES

The invasion of nonnative plant species is one of the primary issues facing land managers today. Invasive species are the second leading threat to endangered species and their habitat, surpassed only by habitat loss. Often introduced from Europe or Asia, they outcompete native species and wreak havoc on natural ecosystems by growing rapidly, seeding prolifically, and reproducing vegetatively. Some species also release

plant toxins into the soil, further reducing native species. Biological controls that keep them in check in their native ranges are often absent in North America.

Examples of invasive species include well-publicized cases like purple loosestrife. Introduced from Europe in the 1700s through shipping ballast water, it spread rapidly through canals and into other suitable wetland habitats. It was also intentionally planted for honey production, and later for landscaping. With a single stem capable of producing over 100,000 seeds annually, it has overrun native vegetation and drastically altered wildlife habitat in more than 40 states, earning it the label "purple plague." Fortunately, a beetle was found in Europe that feeds exclusively on purple loosestrife and provides effective control. The beetle has now been introduced throughout Michigan and other states, and native wetland plants and animals have begun to recover in many areas formerly dominated by purple loosestrife.

Unfortunately, problems with invasive species drastically outweigh success stories. Herbaceous species like garlic mustard (*Alliaria petiolata*) threaten to overtake savanna restorations, and spotted knapweed has already become the "purple plague" of dry prairies. Both species release toxic chemicals into the soil that severely inhibit other plants. Other invasive plants like black swallow-wort (*Vincetoxicum nigrum*) and pale swallow-wort (*V. rossicum*), members of the milkweed family, contain toxic chemicals in leaf tissue. They are shunned by grazing mammals, and even the larvae of the Monarch butterfly fail to develop after feeding on the plants, despite their close relation to other milkweeds. Also known as dog-strangling vines, they grow prolifically in open settings as well as savanna remnants, and quickly smother all other ground vegetation. Once established, swallow-wort is extremely difficult to eradicate.

Invasive shrubs in prairie and savanna settings are equally problematic. In addition to simply outcompeting native plants, they shade out grasses, which reduces the fine fuels needed to carry fires and constrains management options. Many species such as Eurasian honeysuckles and buckthorn have impacts on wildlife as well, including reducing nesting success of songbirds and creating impenetrable thickets

OPPOSITE: Purple loosestrife has been called the "purple plague" of wetlands due to its tendency to displace native plants and destroy wildlife habitat.

of low-quality forage. Other species facilitate alteration of ecosystems through complicated feedback loops. For example, the sprawling canopy of autumn-olive provides protective cover for small mammals like voles, increasing their population. But this in turn leads to drastically higher herbivory rates on oak seedlings and contributes to a lack of oak regeneration in savanna remnants.

Restoration Efforts

Ecological restoration of prairies and savannas is quickly becoming one of the highest priorities for land managers throughout the state. A diverse coalition of groups ranging from federal, state, and local agencies, to universities, nonprofit groups, and individual private landowners, is striving to reverse more than a century of habitat conversion, altered ecological processes, and nonnative species invasions. The result is improved habitat for many rare and declining plants and animals. There is also a growing recognition of the aesthetic and inherent value of prairies and savannas. Showy wildflowers, waving grasses, abundant wildlife, and stately oak trees give us glimpses into our past and opportunities for today. They provide areas for outdoor education, active and passive recreational activities (such as hiking, mountain biking, bird-watching, and hunting), and even spiritual inspiration.

PRESCRIBED FIRE

The most effective tool used to maintain prairies and savannas is prescribed fire. Historically, fire promoted the growth of herbaceous plants, while setting back woody trees and shrubs. In addition, fire has been shown to stimulate grass growth and improve the browse nutrition of native warm-season grasses (species such as big bluestem, little bluestem, Indian grass, and switchgrass that thrive late

OPPOSITE: Black swallow-wort is a rapidly spreading invasive species in Michigan.

Christopher Hoving

in the growing season) while hindering nonnative cool-season grasses (species such as brome and fescue that thrive early in the growing season). Fire can also increase wildflower diversity, depending on the timing and seasonality of the burn. In southern Lower Michigan, fires historically occurred every one to five years, depending on the community type, topography, fuel load, and weather. In most prairies and savannas receiving active management today, prescribed burns are conducted every two to five years. However, each site should be independently evaluated and a management plan developed to meet the restoration goals and objectives. When making management decisions, it is important also to consider the complex nature of the historical fire regime. Sites rarely burned at regular intervals, with fires instead being dictated by variations in the weather from year to year. Therefore, it has been suggested that managers avoid artificially uniform burn intervals, and instead incorporate natural variation in fire frequency that more closely reflects historical conditions.

LEFT: Prescribed burning is used as a management tool to maintain and restore prairies and savannas.

OPPOSITE: Varying the seasonality of prescribed burns from year to year and conducting them during spring, fall, as well as the summer growing season best mimics natural processes and benefits the greatest range of species.

Currently, most prescribed burns are conducted between late March and early May, when humidity is low, winds are light, and fine fuels burn readily. Occasionally, burns are also performed in late fall after plants have mostly senesced. However, appropriate fall burn days with suitably low humidity and light wind can be limited. Historically, many fires in Michigan did occur during spring or fall, especially when started by Native Americans. Lightning-strike fires occurred during the summer as well, but were likely smaller in size. Very few prescribed burns are currently conducted during the growing season, but they may be very effective in stimulating wildflowers, controlling woody species, and maximizing biodiversity. The best approach may be to aim for a combination of spring, fall, and even occasional summer burns over time. This mimics natural patterns and provides a diversity of habitats for the greatest range of species.

Impacts on wildlife are often a concern with prescribed burning. While some wildlife species are fire-adapted and can flee from burns (such as most mammals and birds), other species can be severely affected by fire. Of particular concern are species such as turtles, snakes, and insects, including many species of rare butterflies and moths. Leaving unburned refugia as habitat for wildlife is an important component of habitat management, especially where rare or fire-sensitive species are known to occur. Additionally, the pattern in which a burn is ignited and the rate at which flames spread can be crucial to the survival of some species. In general, slow-moving fires that back-burn into the wind give wildlife the greatest opportunity to escape. In contrast, fast-moving, wind-driven flames and fires that completely encircle an area can easily overrun or trap wildlife attempting to flee. Despite risks to individual animals, burns generally result in habitat improvements that will often yield a much larger benefit to the overall wildlife population. If balanced correctly, prescribed burning can accomplish both goals of improving habitat and minimizing the immediate risk to wildlife.

RESTORING HYDROLOGY

In wet prairies, restoring hydrology may be the most important tool in improving habitat quality and can be used along with prescribed fire to promote diversity and control woody species and invasive plants. In former agricultural fields, breaking old drain tiles can be critical to successful restoration. If a site has been ditched and the water table drastically lowered, filling or plugging the ditch may be necessary before full recovery of the vegetation is possible. Finally, the near extermination of beavers as a result of the fur trade drastically altered wet prairies, prairie fens, and lakeplain prairies. Allowing beavers to return to these areas and construct dams can help restore open conditions to areas that have been colonized by shrubs and trees. It should be noted that mechanical means of restoring hydrology such as breaking drain tiles and filling or plugging ditches requires a great deal of professional expertise and is often costly.

CONTROLLING INVASIVE SPECIES

There are several ways of controlling invasive species. One of the most effective is to restore disrupted ecological processes, such as returning fire to the landscape through prescribed burning, or restoring the hydrology of wetland systems. Mechanical control, either by hand-cutting or brush-hogging with larger equipment, is also utilized, especially when infestations are of sufficient size that prescribed burning and/or hydrologic restoration alone will not be successful. Cutting is more effective when combined with chemical control. Herbicides can be applied to the cut stump in a small but highly concentrated dose. Herbicides can also be applied to resprouts in a more diluted foliar spray. Timing herbicide applications to affect target species when they are most susceptible, while simultaneously minimizing the impact on native species, is critical. Finally, biological control agents have also been effective in controlling some species like purple loosestrife, but years of extensive careful testing are required to ensure they do not spread to other nontarget species or cause other negative impacts.

Chuck Pearson

Chuck Pearson

IVES ROAD FEN

The Ives Road prairie fen is one of the most unique environments in southeast Michigan. Located in Lenawee County, it contains more rare and declining species than nearly any other site in the region. Owned by The Nature Conservancy, it has been the focus of intensive management efforts for many years.

When restoration began, the Ives Road prairie fen faced numerous interrelated problems. Decades of fire suppression and altered hydrology allowed dense thickets of shrubs to invade, shading out grasses, sedges, orchids, and other unique plant species. Deep ditches had been dug through the gently sloping wetland, preventing cold calcareous groundwater from seeping through the soil by diverting it to artificial channels and away from the site. The hydrologic disturbance facilitated a massive invasion by glossy buckthorn, which in turn lowered the water table even further due to its high evapotranspiration rate. Thickets of buckthorn also smothered native plants, including fine-leaved grasses and sedges, making prescribed fire impossible.

Since the early 1990s, The Nature Conservancy has worked tirelessly to restore this important harbor of biodiversity. With the help of hundreds of volunteers, thousands of hours were spent cutting and applying herbicide to glossy buckthorn. When dense carpets of buckthorn seedlings sprouted from the seed bank, Nature Conservancy staff scorched them with hand-held propane torches, simultaneously eliminating the seedlings and stimulating native plants. As grasses and sedges recolonized, they provided the fine fuels necessary for land managers to conduct prescribed burns and restore fire to the ecosystem at a larger scale. Finally, earth-moving equipment was carefully brought in to the site to fill in ditches in an attempt to restore hydrology. Over 325 feet (100 meters) of drainage tiles were also removed manually.

The restoration efforts have paid off. Groundwater levels have risen with the improved hydrology and removal of glossy buckthorn. Native plants and wildflowers have rebounded, and rare animals are once again thriving in restored sections of the fen. Recently, a flower previously thought to be extirpated in Michigan was rediscovered in adjacent habitat, further highlighting the significance of restoration efforts at this site. There is still much work to be done, and stewards continue efforts to remove invasive species, conduct prescribed burns, and sponsor regular volunteer workdays. Thanks to these efforts, the Ives Road prairie fen will continue to be a harbor of biodiversity for generations to come.

TOP: A sign welcomes visitors to the Ives Road Fen Preserve, owned by The Nature Conservancy.

BOTTOM: Volunteers help restore Ives Road prairie fen by removing thickets of invasive species.

PRAIRIE PLANTING

Prairie planting, also called prairie creation or reconstruction, attempts to reverse habitat loss by planting native prairie species, often on recently abandoned or marginal agricultural land. As grasses and wildflowers establish, they provide habitat for a myriad of species, especially grassland songbirds as well as game birds such as ring-necked pheasant. Prairie plantings also benefit rivers and streams. Native grasses and wildflowers contain deep root systems, allowing them to soak up rainwater, filter excess nutrients, and minimize soil erosion. Planting prairie species may also be used in the restoration of remnants that already contain an assemblage of native plants. Often, a remnant might first be treated with a prescribed burn, which will lead to a flush of species present in the seed bank. But if key species remain absent after several years of prescribed burns and other restoration work, seeding may be necessary to restore biodiversity. Savanna creation is much less commonly practiced, but as recognition of the importance of these rare communities grows, it may increase in popularity.

Although prairie species can be established in virtually any type of open ground, it is important to recognize the ecological and landscape context of a site. A planted prairie adjacent to a remnant community such as a prairie fen or oak barrens provides a better representation of the historical

Treating the stumps of woody shrubs with a concentrated herbicide immediately after cutting reduces or eliminates resprouting.

Dave Kenyon

INTERNATIONAL
656

landscape pattern, and will likely be of more use to rare and declining wildlife species than a prairie planted near a beech-maple forest. Restoration at a larger scale might involve planting a prairie and gradually also restoring more open conditions to an adjacent closed-canopy former savanna through prescribed burning and thinning. At a small scale, however, prairie plantings of virtually any size and type will have benefits, even if it is only to attract insects to a small butterfly garden and to reduce rainwater runoff from lawns and adjacent hard surfaces. Seeds and plugs for prairie planting are available from a variety of sources, ranging from local native plant nurseries to large commercial vendors in other states.

In general, plants collected from local sources are preferred because they are more likely to be of similar genotypes as plants growing naturally in nearby remnant habitats. In contrast, plants originating from sources hundreds of miles away are more likely to be of different genotypes, and pose a risk of genetic contamination to local members of the same species as a result of interbreeding. Furthermore, because nonlocal genotypes are not adapted to local conditions, they tend be less competitive than local genotypes. As a general rule of thumb, local sources may be more appropriate than sources elsewhere in the state, which in turn are preferred to other sources at similar latitudes in the Great Lakes basin (such as Minnesota or Wisconsin), or even more remote places like Iowa or Nebraska. Always ask a grower about the original seed source, since local nurseries may simply resell plants from other, more distant suppliers. Another issue is that many native species are sold as cultivars, which are often more robust and vigorous than naturally occurring varieties of the same species. If established on the natural landscape, cultivars may outcompete local genotypes. Factors other than distance may also affect seed source choices. Many prairie species have broad ranges, occur in multiple habitats, and may have different genotypes that are adapted to different environmental conditions. Thus, it may also be important to match the moisture and soil type of a site with seeds that originate in similar conditions. In the end, selecting the right genotype and even species is a complex decision that must be made by considering a wide variety of factors, including but not

OPPOSITE: Planting prairie seeds with a no-till drill is one way of quickly establishing prairie habitat.

limited to availability, relative cost of local versus more remote sources, and the goals and potential impacts of the project (such as proximity to remnants, difficulty of plant establishment, etc.). Overall, no hard and fast rules can be made, and there is a need for more research on this somewhat controversial topic.

What You Can Do

The majority of prairie and savanna remnants are in private ownership, and private landowners play a vital role in their conservation, restoration, and management. The future of these beautiful, dynamic systems depends on individuals restoring habitat on private land, planting prairies or wildflower gardens where appropriate, and volunteering with numerous local land conservancies and conservation organizations. The following are some activities that you can engage in to promote prairie and savanna natural communities:

- Restore remnant habitats on your property.
- Learn to recognize invasive species and remove them from your property. Techniques vary for each species and site. For more information, consult an expert or refer to publications under Management in appendix 3.
- Landscape with native species, and consider planting a butterfly garden or demonstration prairie. Many local County Conservation Districts sponsor native plant sales, and the Michigan Native Plant Producers Association (MNPPA) also lists many local native plant nurseries. For more information visit the MNPPA website.
- If eligible and able, participate in federal programs like the Conservation Reserve Program (CRP) or Wildlife Habitat Incentives Program (WHIP), restoring former cropland or fallow fields to prairie or

OPPOSITE: Native wildflowers are often hardier, require less watering, and attract more beneficial insects and butterflies than traditional landscaping species, many of which are European or Asian in origin.

savanna. Information on these programs is available through local offices of the Farm Service Agency (for CRP) and Natural Resource Conservation Service (for WHIP).

- Consider participating in the Michigan Department of Natural Resources (DNR) Wildlife Division's Landowner Incentive Program, which provides assistance to property owners interested in managing their land as habitat for rare species. The program especially focuses on prairie fens, prairies, and savannas.
- Volunteer with conservation organizations like Michigan State Parks, The Nature Conservancy, Michigan Nature Association, local land conservancies, and other conservation organizations (see appendix 4 for contact information).
- If you believe you may have high-quality habitat on your property, consider a conservation easement. The Nature Conservancy and many local land conservancies can assist with permanent protection of sensitive habitats while you retain legal ownership. Conservation easements may also result in substantially lower property tax burdens.

Prairies and savannas are important parts of our natural heritage. They were the setting for some of the earliest inland settlements in our state, the sites of college campuses and cemeteries, and even the foundation of names for counties, townships, villages, and roads. They exist today in tiny tattered patches, awaiting conservation and restoration by concerned citizens, organizations, and agencies. They serve as natural open space, important habitat for rare species, areas for recreation, sites for educational study, and places of spiritual inspiration. Prairies and savannas are a reminder of our past heritage and an inspiration for our future, in hopes that they may continue to grace our landscape for generations to come.

OPPOSITE: A volunteer collects native prairie seed at a state park stewardship workday.

APPENDIX 1

Rare and Declining Animal Species Found in Prairies and Savannas

SCIENTIFIC NAME	COMMON NAME	STATUS	PRAIRIE	SAVANNA
Amphibians				
Acris crepitans blanchardi	Blanchard's cricket frog	T	■	
Ambystoma laterale	Blue-spotted salamander		■	■
Ambystoma texanum	Smallmouth salamander	E	■	■
Ambystoma tigrinum tigrinum	Eastern tiger salamander		■	■
Bufo fowleri	Fowler's toad		■	■
Rana palustris	Pickerel frog		■	
Rana pipiens	Northern leopard frog	SC	■	■
Birds				
Accipiter cooperii	Cooper's hawk			■
Accipiter gentilis	Northern goshawk	SC		■
Ammodramus henslowii	Henslow's sparrow	E	■	

KEY
E = state endangered
T = state threatened
SC = state special concern
LE = federal endangered
C = candidate for federal listing

SCIENTIFIC NAME	COMMON NAME	STATUS	PRAIRIE	SAVANNA
Ammodramus savannarum	Grasshopper sparrow	SC	■	■
Anas discors	Blue-winged teal		■	■
Anas rubripes	American black duck		■	
Asio flammeus	Short-eared owl	E	■	■
Bartramia longicauda	Upland sandpiper		■	
Botaurus lentiginosus	American bittern	SC	■	
Chordeiles minor	Common nighthawk			■
Circus cyaneus	Northern harrier	SC	■	
Cistothorus platensis	Sedge wren		■	■
Coccyzus americanus	Yellow-billed cuckoo			■
Colaptes auratus	Northern flicker			■
Colinus virginianus	Northern bobwhite		■	■
Dendroica discolor	Prairie warbler	E	■	■
Dendroica kirtlandii	Kirtland's warbler	E, LE		■
Dolichonyx oryzivorus	Bobolink		■	■
Empidonax minimus	Least flycatcher			■
Falco columbarius	Merlin	T		■
Lanius excubitor	Northern shrike			■
Lanius ludovicianus migrans	Migrant loggerhead shrike	E		■
Melanerpes erythrocephalus	Red-headed woodpecker		■	■
Mimus polyglottos	Northern mockingbird			■
Passerculus sandwichensis	Savanna sparrow		■	■

SCIENTIFIC NAME	COMMON NAME	STATUS	PRAIRIE	SAVANNA
Pipilo erythrophthalmus	Eastern towhee			■
Pooecetes gramineus	Vesper sparrow		■	■
Progne subis	Purple martin		■	■
Spiza americana	Dickcissel	SC	■	■
Spizella pusilla	Field sparrow		■	■
Sturnella magna	Eastern meadowlark		■	
Sturnella neglecta	Western meadowlark	SC	■	■
Toxostoma rufum	Brown thrasher			■
Tympanuchus phasianellus	Sharp-tailed grouse	SC	■	■
Tyrannus tyrannus	Eastern kingbird		■	■
Tyto alba	Barn owl	E	■	
Insects				
BEETLES				
Nicrophorus americanus	American burying beetle	E, LE	■	
BUTTERFLIES AND MOTHS				
Atrytonopsis hianna	Dusted skipper	SC	■	■
Battus philenor	Pipevine swallowtail	SC		■
Brachionycha borealis	Boreal fan moth	SC		■
Callophrys henrici	Henry's elfin	T		■
Callophrys irus	Frosted elfin	T	■	■
Catocala amestris	Three-staff underwing	E	■	■
Catocala dulciola	Quiet underwing	SC		■

KEY
E = state endangered
T = state threatened
SC = state special concern
LE = federal endangered
C = candidate for federal listing

SCIENTIFIC NAME	COMMON NAME	STATUS	PRAIRIE	SAVANNA
Chlosyne gorgone carlota	Gorgone checkerspot	SC	■	■
Erynnis baptisiae	Wild indigo duskywing	SC	■	■
Erynnis persius persius	Persius duskywing	T	■	■
Fixsenia favonius ontario	Northern hairstreak	SC		■
Hemileuca maia	Barrens buckmoth	SC		■
Hesperia ottoe	Ottoe skipper	T	■	■
Lycaeides melissa samuelis	Karner blue	T, LE	■	■
Merolonche dolli	Doll's merolonche	SC		■
Meropleon ambifusca	Newman's brocade	SC	■	
Neonympha mitchellii mitchellii	Mitchell's satyr	E, LE	■	
Oarisma poweshiek	Poweshiek skipperling	T	■	
Papaipema beeriana	Blazing star borer	SC	■	■
Papaipema cerina	Golden borer	SC	■	
Papaipema maritima	Maritime sunflower borer	SC	■	
Papaipema sciata	Culver's root borer	SC	■	
Papaipema silphii	Silphium borer moth	T	■	
Papaipema speciosissima	Regal fern borer	SC	■	
Phyciodes batesii	Tawny crescent	SC		■
Pygarctia spraguei	Sprague's pygarctia	SC	■	■
Pyrgus wyandot	Grizzled skipper	SC		■
Schinia indiana	Phlox moth	E	■	■
Schina lucens	Leadplant flower moth	E	■	■

SCIENTIFIC NAME	COMMON NAME	STATUS	PRAIRIE	SAVANNA
Spartiniphaga inops	Spartina borer moth	SC	■	
Speyeria idalia	Regal fritillary	E	■	■
CICADAS AND HOPPERS				
Dorydiella kansana	A leafhopper	SC	■	
Flexamia delongi	A leafhopper	SC	■	
Flexamia huroni	Huron River leafhopper	T	■	
Flexamia reflexus	A leafhopper	SC		■
Lepyronia angulifera	Angular spittlebug	SC	■	
Lepyronia gibbosa	Great Plains spittlebug	SC	■	■
Philaenarcys killa	A spittlebug		■	■
Prosapia ignipectus	Red-legged spittlebug	SC	■	■
GRASSHOPPERS AND CRICKETS				
Appalachia arcana	Secretive locust	SC	■	■
Atlanticus davisi	Davis's shield-bearer	SC		■
Melanoplus eurycercus	A spur-throat grasshopper			■
Melanoplus flavidus	Blue-legged locust	SC	■	■
Melanoplus viridipes	Hebard's green-legged locust			■
Neoconocephalus retusus	Conehead grasshopper	SC		■
Oecanthus laricis	Tamarack tree cricket		■	
Orchelimum delicatum	Delicate meadow katydid	SC	■	
Orphulella pelidna pelidna	Barrens locust	SC	■	■
Psinidia fenestralis fenestralis	Atlantic-coast locust	SC		■

KEY E = state endangered
T = state threatened
SC = state special concern
LE = federal endangered
C = candidate for federal listing

SCIENTIFIC NAME	COMMON NAME	STATUS	PRAIRIE	SAVANNA
Mammals				
Clethrionomys gapperi	Southern red-backed vole			■
Cryptotis parva	Least shrew	T	■	■
Microtus ochrogaster	Prairie vole	E		■
Microtus pinetorum	Woodland vole	SC		■
Mustela nivalis	Least weasel		■	
Myotis sodalis	Indiana bat	E, LE	■	■
Peromyscus maniculatus gracilis	Deer mouse			■
Synaptomys cooperi	Southern bog lemming			■
Reptiles				
Apidoscelis sexlineatus	Six-lined racerunner	SC	■	■
Clemmys guttata	Spotted turtle	T	■	■
Clonophis kirtlandii	Kirtland's snake	E	■	
Coluber constrictor foxii	Blue racer		■	■
Elaphe vulpina goldi	Eastern fox snake	T	■	
Elaphe obsoleta obsoleta	Black rat snake	SC	■	■
Emydoidea blandingii	Blanding's turtle	SC	■	■
Heterodon platirhinos	Eastern hognose snake		■	■
Liochlorophis vernalis	Smooth green snake		■	■
Sistrurus catenatus catenatus	Eastern massasauga	SC, C	■	■
Terrapene carolina carolina	Eastern box turtle	SC	■	■

Rare and Declining Plant Species Found in Prairies and Savannas

SCIENTIFIC NAME	COMMON NAME	STATUS	WET TO WET-MESIC	MESIC TO DRY-MESIC	DRY
Agalinis gattingeri	Gattinger's gerardia	E	■		■
Agalinis skinneriana	Skinner's gerardia	E	■		
Agoseris glauca	Prairie or Pale agoseris	T			■
Amorpha canescens	Leadplant	SC			■
Androsace occidentalis	Rock-jasmine	E			■
Angelica venenosa	Hairy angelica	SC		■	
Arabis missouriensis var. deamii	Missouri rock-cress	SC			■
Aristida dichotoma	Shinner's three-awned grass	X			■
Aristida longespica	Three-awned grass	T	■		
Aristida tuberculosa	Beach three-awned grass	E			■
Artemisia ludoviciana	Western mugwort	T			■

KEY
E = state endangered
T = state threatened
SC = state special concern
X = state extirpated
LT = federal threatened

SCIENTIFIC NAME	COMMON NAME	STATUS	WET TO WET-MESIC	MESIC TO DRY-MESIC	DRY
Asclepias hirtella	Tall green milkweed	T	■	■	
Asclepias ovalifolia	Dwarf milkweed	E			■
Asclepias purpurascens	Purple milkweed	T	■	■	
Asclepias sullivantii	Sullivant's milkweed	T	■		
Aster praealtus	Willow aster	SC	■		
Aster sericeus	Western silvery aster	T			■
Astragalus canadensis	Canadian milk-vetch	T			■
Astragalus neglectus	Cooper's milk-vetch	SC			■
Baptisia lactea	Prairie false indigo	SC		■	
Baptisia leucophaea	Cream wild indigo	E			■
Bartonia paniculata	Panicled screw-stem	T	■		
Berula erecta	Cut-leaved water-parsnip	T	■		
Besseya bullii	Kitten-tails	E		■	
Botrychium pallidum	Pale moonwort	SC			■
Bouteloua curtipendula	Side-oats grama grass	E		■	■
Cacalia plantaginea	Prairie Indian-plantain	SC	■		
Calamagrostis stricta	Narrow-leaved reedgrass	T	■		
Carex festucacea	Fescue sedge	SC	■		
Carex gravida	Sedge	X			■
Carex richardsonii	Richardson's sedge	SC			■
Celtis tenuifolia	Dwarf hackberry	SC			■

SCIENTIFIC NAME	COMMON NAME	STATUS	WET TO WET-MESIC	MESIC TO DRY-MESIC	DRY
Cirsium hillii	Hill's thistle	SC			■
Coreopsis palmata	Prairie coreopsis	T		■	
Corydalis flavula	Yellow fumewort	T		■	
Cuscuta indecora	Dodder	SC			■
Cuscuta pentagona	Dodder	SC			■
Cypripedium candidum	White lady-slipper	T	■		
Dalea purpurea	Purple prairie-clover	X			■
Dasistoma macrophylla	Mullein foxglove	E			■
Digitaria filiformis	Slender finger-grass	X			■
Dodecatheon meadia	Shooting-star	E	■	■	
Draba reptans	Creeping whitlow-grass	T		■	
Drosera anglica	English sundew	SC	■		
Echinacea purpurea	Purple coneflower	X		■	
Eleocharis engelmannii	Engelmann's spike-rush	SC	■		
Eleocharis tricostata	Three-ribbed spike-rush	T	■		
Eragrostis capillaris	Love grass	SC			■
Eryngium yuccifolium	Rattlesnake-master	T	■		■
Festuca scabrella	Rough fescue	T			■
Filipendula rubra	Queen-of-the-prairie	T	■		
Fimbristylis puberula	Chestnut sedge	X	■		
Gentiana flavida	White gentian	E		■	■

KEY
E = state endangered
T = state threatened
SC = state special concern
X = state extirpated
LT = federal threatened

SCIENTIFIC NAME	COMMON NAME	STATUS	WET TO WET-MESIC	MESIC TO DRY-MESIC	DRY
Gentiana puberulenta	Downy gentian	E			■
Gentiana saponaria	Soapwort gentian	X			■
Geum triflorum	Prairie-smoke	T			■
Gillenia trifoliata	Bowman's root	E			■
Gratiola virginiana	Round-fruited hedge hyssop	T	■		
Helianthus hirsutus	Whiskered sunflower	SC	■		■
Helianthus microcephalus	Small wood sunflower	X		■	■
Helianthus mollis	Downy sunflower	T		■	■
Hieracium paniculatum	Panicled hawkweed	T			■
Hypericum gentianoides	Gentian-leaved St. John's-wort	SC	■		
Ipomoea pandurata	Wild potato-vine	T			■
Juncus vaseyi	Vasey's rush	T	■		
Kuhnia eupatorioides	False boneset	SC			■
Lactuca floridana	Woodland lettuce	T			■
Lechea minor	Least pinweed	X			■
Lespedeza procumbens	Trailing bush-clover	X			■
Leucospora multifida	Conobea	SC	■		
Liatris punctata	Dotted blazing-star	X			■
Linum sulcatum	Furrowed flax	SC			■
Linum virginianum	Virginia flax	T			■
Lithospermum incisum	Narrow-leaved puccoon	X			■

SCIENTIFIC NAME	COMMON NAME	STATUS	WET TO WET-MESIC	MESIC TO DRY-MESIC	DRY
Lycopodiella margueriteae	Northern prostrate clubmoss	T	■		
Muhlenbergia richardsonis	Mat muhly	T	■		
Onosmodium molle	Marbleweed	X		■	■
Oryzopsis canadensis	Canada rice-grass	T			■
Oxalis violacea	Violet wood-sorrel	X	■	■	
Panicum leibergii	Leiberg's panic-grass	T		■	■
Panicum polyanthes	Round-seed panic grass	E	■		
Paronychia fastigiata	Low-forked chickweed	X			■
Penstemon calycosus	Smooth beardtongue	T			■
Penstemon gracilis	Slender beardtongue	E			■
Penstemon pallidus	Pale beardtongue	SC			■
Phaseolus polystachios	Wild bean	X		■	
Phlox bifida	Cleft phlox	X			■
Phlox maculata	Spotted phlox	T	■		
Platanthera leucophaea	Eastern prairie fringed orchid	E, LT	■		
Polemonium reptans	Jacob's ladder	T	■		
Polygala cruciata	Cross-leaved milkwort	SC	■		
Polygala incarnata	Pink milkwort	X	■	■	■
Polytaenia nuttallii	Prairie-parsley	X		■	
Prunus alleghaniensis var. davisii	Alleghany plum	SC			■
Pycnanthemum pilosum	Hairy mountain-mint	T		■	

KEY
E = state endangered
T = state threatened
SC = state special concern
X = state extirpated
LT = federal threatened

SCIENTIFIC NAME	COMMON NAME	STATUS	WET TO WET-MESIC	MESIC TO DRY-MESIC	DRY
Ranunculus rhomboideus	Prairie buttercup	T		■	
Rhynchospora macrostachya	Tall beak-rush	SC	■		
Rudbeckia subtomentosa	Sweet coneflower	X	■	■	
Ruellia humilis	Hairy ruellia	T		■	■
Sanguisorba canadensis	Canadian burnet	E	■		
Scirpus clintonii	Clinton's bulrush	SC	■		
Scleria pauciflora	Few-flowered nut-rush	E	■		■
Scleria triglomerata	Tall nut-rush	SC	■	■	■
Scutellaria incana	Downy skullcap	X			■
Scutellaria parvula	Small skullcap	T		■	
Silene stellata	Starry campion	T			■
Silene virginica	Fire pink	E			■
Silphium integrifolium	Rosinweed	T		■	
Silphium laciniatum	Compass-plant	T		■	
Sisyrinchium atlanticum	Atlantic blue-eyed-grass	T	■		
Sisyrinchium farwellii	Farwell's blue-eyed-grass	X		■	
Sisyrinchium strictum	Blue-eyed-grass	SC		■	
Solidago bicolor	White goldenrod	E			■
Solidago missouriensis	Missouri goldenrod	T			■
Spiranthes ovalis	Lesser ladies'-tresses	T		■	
Sporobolus clandestinus	Dropseed	E			■

SCIENTIFIC NAME	COMMON NAME	STATUS	WET TO WET-MESIC	MESIC TO DRY-MESIC	DRY
Sporobolus heterolepis	Prairie dropseed	SC	■	■	
Strophostyles helvula	Trailing wild bean	SC		■	
Tomanthera auriculata	Eared false foxglove	X		■	
Tradescantia bracteata	Long-bracted spiderwort	X			■
Tradescantia virginiana	Virginia spiderwort	SC			■
Trichostema brachiatum	False pennyroyal	T			■
Trichostema dichotomum	Bastard pennyroyal	T			■
Triplasis purpurea	Sand grass	SC			■
Vaccinium cespitosum	Dwarf bilberry	T			■
Valeriana edulis var. ciliata	Edible valerian	T	■		
Viola novae-angliae	New England violet	T		■	
Viola pedatifida	Prairie birdfoot violet	T		■	
Zizia aptera	Prairie golden alexanders	T		■	

KEY
E = state endangered
T = state threatened
SC = state special concern
X = state extirpated
LT = federal threatened

APPENDIX 3

Recommended Reading

MICHIGAN PRAIRIE AND SAVANNA NATURAL COMMUNITIES

Chapman, K. A. and R. Brewer. 2008. Prairie and Savanna in Southern Lower Michigan: History, Classification, Ecology. *The Michigan Botanist* 47:1–48.

Kost, M. A., D. A. Albert, J. G. Cohen, B. S. Slaughter, R. K. Schillo, C. R. Weber, and K. A. Chapman. 2007. *Natural Communities of Michigan: Classification and Description*. Report No. 2007–21. Lansing: Michigan Natural Features Inventory. 319 pp.

WET AND WET-MESIC PRAIRIES AND SAVANNAS

Albert D. A., and M. A. Kost. 1998. Natural Community Abstract for Lakeplain Wet-Mesic Prairie. Lansing: Michigan Natural Features Inventory. 4 pp.

———. 1998. Natural Community Abstract for Lakeplain Wet Prairie. Lansing: Michigan Natural Features Inventory. 4 pp.

Cohen, J. G. 2001. Natural Community Abstract for Lakeplain Oak Openings. Lansing: Michigan Natural Features Inventory. 9 pp.

Spieles, J. B., P. J. Comer, D. A. Albert, and M. A. Kost. 1999. Natural Community Abstract for Prairie Fen. Lansing: Michigan Natural Features Inventory. 4 pp.

MESIC AND DRY-MESIC PRAIRIES AND SAVANNAS

Cohen, J. G. 2001. Natural Community Abstract for Lakeplain Oak Openings. Lansing: Michigan Natural Features Inventory. 9 pp.

———. 2004. Natural Community Abstract for Bur Oak Plains. Lansing: Michigan Natural Features Inventory. 13 pp.

———. 2004. Natural Community Abstract for Oak Openings. Lansing: Michigan Natural Features Inventory. 13 pp.

Kost, M. A. 2004. Natural Community Abstract for Dry-Mesic Prairie. Lansing: Michigan Natural Features Inventory. 8 pp.

———. 2004. Natural Community Abstract for Mesic Prairie. Lansing: Michigan Natural Features Inventory. 10 pp.

DRY PRAIRIES AND SAVANNAS

Cohen, J. G. 2000. Natural Community Abstract for Oak-Pine Barrens. Lansing: Michigan Natural Features Inventory. 6 pp.

———. 2001. Natural Community Abstract for Oak Barrens. Lansing: Michigan Natural Features Inventory. 8 pp.

Comer, P. J. 1996. Natural Community Abstract for Pine Barrens. Lansing: Michigan Natural Features Inventory. 3 pp.

Kost, M. A. 2004. Natural Community Abstract for Dry Sand Prairie. Lansing: Michigan Natural Features Inventory. 9 pp.

MANAGEMENT

Czarapata, E. J. 2005. *Invasive Plants of the Upper Midwest: An Illustrated Guide to Their Identification and Control.* Madison: University of Wisconsin Press. 215 pp.

Element Stewardship Abstracts [on the Control of Invasive Species]. Arlington, Va.: The Nature Conservancy, http://tncweeds.ucdavis.edu/esadocs.html.

O'Connor, R. 2006. *A Land Manager's Guide to Prairies and Savannas in Michigan: History, Classification and Management.* Report No. 2006-18. Lansing: Michigan Natural Features Inventory. 58 pp.

Packard, S., and C. F. Mutel, eds. 1997. *The Tallgrass Restoration Handbook: For Prairies, Savannas, and Woodlands.* Washington, D.C.: Island Press. 463 pp.

Tu, M., C. Hurd, and J. M. Randall. 2001. Weed Control Methods Handbook: Tools and Techniques for Use in Natural Areas. The Nature Conservancy, http://tncweeds.ucdavis.edu/handbook.html.

Organizations and Agencies Involved with Prairie and Savanna Conservation in Michigan

- **Headwaters Land Conservancy**, 110 S. Elm St., Gaylord, MI 49735; (989) 731-0573; otsego.org/hwlc. REGION: northeast Lower Michigan
- **Kalamazoo Nature Center,** 7000 N. Westnedge Ave., Kalamazoo, MI 49009; (269) 381-1574; www.naturecenter.org. REGION: Kalamazoo County
- **Land Conservancy of West Michigan**, 1345 Monroe Ave. NW, Ste. 324, Grand Rapids, MI 49505; (616) 451-9476; www.naturenearby.org. REGION: central west Michigan
- **The Livingston Land Conservancy**, P.O. Box 236, Brighton, MI 48116-0236; (810) 229-3290; livingstonlandconservancy.org. REGION: Livingston County
- **Michigan Audubon Society,** 6011 W. St. Joseph, P.O. Box 80527, Lansing, MI 48908-0527; (517) 886-9144; www.michiganaudubon.org. REGION: statewide
- **Michigan Conservation Districts,** www.macd.org. REGION: statewide by county
- **Michigan Nature Association,** 326 E. Grand River Ave., Williamston, MI 48895; (517) 655-5655; www.michigannature.org. REGION: statewide

- **Michigan State Park Stewardship Program,** www.michigan.gov/dnrvolunteers. REGION: southern Lower Michigan
- **The Nature Conservancy,** Michigan Field Office, 101 East Grand River, Lansing, MI 48906; (517) 316-0300; www.nature.org. REGION: statewide
- **North Oakland Headwaters Land Conservancy,** P.O. Box 285, Clarkston, MI 48347; (248) 846-6547; www.nohlc.org. REGION: northwest Oakland County
- **Raisin Valley Land Trust,** 1042 Sutton Road, Suite 3, Adrian, MI 49221; (517) 265-5599; www.rvlt.org. REGION: River Raisin watershed (portions of Hillsdale, Jackson, Lenawee, Monroe, and Washtenaw counties)
- **Southeast Michigan Land Conservancy**, 8383 Vreeland Road, Superior Township, MI 48198; (734) 484-6565; www.smlcland.org. REGION: southeast Lower Michigan
- **Southwest Michigan Land Conservancy,** 6851 S. Sprinkle Road, Portage, MI 49002; (269) 324-1600; swmlc.org. REGION: southwest Lower Michigan
- **The Stewardship Network**, 416 Longshore Drive, Ann Arbor, MI 48105; (734) 996-3190; www.stewardshipnetwork.org. REGION: statewide by regional clusters
- **Washtenaw Land Trust,** 1100 N. Main St., Ann Arbor, MI 48104; (734) 302-5263; washtenawlandtrust.org. REGION: Washtenaw, Jackson, and Ingham counties

INCENTIVE PROGRAMS FOR PRIVATE LANDOWNERS

- **Conservation Reserve Program (CRP) & Conservation Reserve Enhancement Program (CREP),** USDA Farm Services Agency; www.fsa.usda.gov/FSA. REGION: statewide by county offices
- **Landowner Incentive Program (LIP),** Michigan Department of Natural Resources–Wildlife Division; michigan.gov/dnrlip. REGION: statewide

- **Partners for Wildlife,** U.S. Fish and Wildlife Service; http://ecos.fws.gov/partners. REGION: statewide
- **Wildlife Habitat Incentives Program (WHIP),** Natural Resource Conservation Service; www.mi.nrcs.usda.gov/programs/whip.html. REGION: statewide

Glossary

Allelopathy: the chemical inhibition of one organism by another.

Awn: a thin, elongated, needle-like projection from a seed or other portion of the fruit of a plant.

Barrens: a generic term usually referring to dry savannas and occasionally dry prairies. In Michigan, there are several natural community types that fall under the category of dry savanna or barrens, including oak barrens, oak-pine barrens, and pine barrens.

Biodiversity: the variety and abundance of species, their genetic composition, and the natural communities, ecosystems, and landscapes in which they occur.

Calcareous: composed of or containing calcium carbonate, a mineral with a high pH. Often used to describe alkaline soil or groundwater.

Circumneutral: having a pH around neutral, or 7.0.

Cool-season grass: a grass that completes most of its growth during spring and early summer. Examples include native species such as wild-rye (*Elymus* spp.), as well as many nonnative species such as Kentucky bluegrass, brome, and fescue.

Cultivar: a variety of a plant species intentionally bred and propagated through horticultural techniques, often having specific traits not normally found in the natural environment.

Dry-mesic: an ecological term for describing a site or natural community with soil characteristics that make it slightly too dry for ideal plant growth, but not extremely dry.

Ecological restoration: the process of returning a site that has been degraded by changes to its biotic or abiotic components to a more natural state, usually through the removal of invasive species and the reestablishment of natural processes like hydrology or periodic fires.

Ecosystem: an ecological system composed of biotic (plants, animals, microorganisms, etc.) and abiotic (air, water, soil, etc.) parts.

Elaiosome: an oil-filled projection on a seed or fruit, often functioning to attract dispersal agents such as ants.

Endangered: a species or community in danger of extinction, either statewide (state endangered), nationally (federally endangered), or globally (globally endangered). Usually refers to a species legally protected from intentional destruction on an official list, as designated by a state or federal authority. When used to refer to a natural community or ecosystem, it implies extreme rarity but not legal protection.

Esker: a glacial landform characterized as a narrow winding ridge, deposited from sediment laid down along the path of an ancient river flowing beneath glacial ice.

Evapotranspiration: the process of water evaporating through pores in the surface of a plant leaf.

Fine fuel: natural fuels such as grasses, sedges, and oak leaves that easily catch fire and allow flames to spread.

Fire frequency: how often a fire occurs on a given site or in a particular natural community.

Fire intensity: the heat energy released in a fire. Often confused with fire severity, or the damage caused by a fire to woody vegetation or soil.

Fire regime: the frequency, intensity, and type of fires that occur in a particular natural community or ecosystem.

Fire suppression: the prevention or immediate extinction of a fire; a policy of putting out fires wherever and whenever they occur regardless of their potential harm or benefit.

Firebreak: a strip of ground cleared of flammable vegetation, intended to keep a fire from spreading beyond that point.

Forb: a generic term for broad-leaved plants.

G-rank: the numerical rank given to a species or natural community to describe its rarity on a global basis. Ranges from 1 to 5, with 1 being extremely rare and 5 being very common.

Genotype: the genetic makeup of an organism. Often used to describe an individual plant or seed that originated in a particular area, and is therefore more likely to be adapted to certain conditions.

Girdle: damage that completely encircles the main stem of a tree, killing all wood above the damaged point; may be caused by cankers, rodent feeding, mechanical injury, etc.

Grassland: a generic term describing an area dominated by grasses, including natural prairies and savannas as well as planted fields.

Herbaceous: a plant without woody tissue, instead initiating new growth from the ground and dying back every year.

Heterogeneous: having a diverse or irregular composition, usually referring to an assemblage of species, communities, or landforms in a particular area.

High Plains region: a region of central northern Lower Michigan relatively high in elevation and characterized by flat, sandy terrain.

Hydrology: the study of the properties, distribution, and effects of water on the earth's surface and in the soil.

Hygroscopic: capable of easily absorbing moisture.

Interlobate region: a region of southern Lower Michigan with a diverse assemblage of landforms deposited at the boundaries of large lobes of glacial ice.

Invasive species: a species that does not naturally occur in a specific area and whose introduction causes or is likely to cause economic or environmental harm or harm to human health.

Kame: a glacial landform characterized as a rounded, steep-sided hill formed by blocks of melting glacial ice, usually with soils comprised of a mixture of sand, silt, clay, and gravel.

Keystone species: species that have a key role in the ecosystem, often altering conditions and benefiting other species in a unique and significant manner through their activities. They often have a disproportionate effect relative to their abundance.

Lakeplain: a glacial landform formed by large bodies of water, such as the precursors to the Great Lakes, and comprised of low, flat areas formed by standing water (often with heavy silt and clay soils) and higher sandy ridges formed by ancient beaches.

Landform: a feature on the landscape; in Michigan, usually of glacial origin. Examples include moraines, outwash channels, outwash plains, kames, eskers, and lakeplains.

Loam: soil with an equal mixture of sand, silt, and clay, usually ideal for plant growth both in terms of water-holding capacity and nutrient availability.

Marl: soft calcium carbonate mixed with clay, usually white to light gray in color, typically precipitated out of highly alkaline water in freshwater lakes and ponds.

Mast: fruits or nuts used as a food source by wildlife.

Mesic: a site or community that is intermediate in moisture availability, being neither too wet nor too dry, and often ideal for plant growth.

Moraine: a glacial landform deposited either at the stagnating terminal margin of ice, producing a large hill (end moraine) or deposited as a broad ice sheet melts in place, forming a rolling plain (ground moraine). Moraines are characterized by an unsorted mixture of sand, silt, and clay soil particles, the proportion being determined by what types of sediments the glacier was carrying at the time of deposition.

Native: a species that occurs naturally in a specific area, and is usually adapted to local or regional ecological conditions.

Natural community: an assemblage of species naturally occurring on the landscape, grouped together by adaptations to a common environmental condition, such as a particular moisture regime, soil characteristics, or sunlight requirement. The Michigan Natural Features Inventory recognizes 76 distinct natural community types in the state.

Nonnative species: a species that does not naturally occur in a local or regional area (such as Michigan or North America). Also sometimes termed alien species. Nonnative species may or may not be invasive, depending on their ability to adapt to local conditions and compete with other species.

Oak grubs: shrubby oak trees with a large root system caused by being repeatedly top-killed by fire.

Oak openings: a dry-mesic savanna natural community. Also historically used to describe a region in southern Lower Michigan and northwest Ohio where these communities were formerly abundant.

Outwash channel: a glacial landform characterized as a relatively narrow, flat plain deposited by a glacial river. Soils are usually well-sorted sands, sometimes now overlain by accumulated peat in wetland environments.

Outwash plain: a glacial landform characterized as a broad, flat to slightly rolling plain deposited by large sheets of glacial meltwater. Soils are usually well-sorted sands.

Peat: organic matter slowly decomposing due to saturated conditions and therefore a lack of oxygen. Often used to describe organic soils in a wetland environment.

pH: a measure of acidity, ranging from 0 (strongly acidic) to 14 (strongly basic or alkaline) on a logarithmic scale, with 7.0 being neutral.

Prairie: a generic term describing an area with few, if any, trees, usually dominated by grasses and broad-leaved herbaceous plants.

Prairie fen: a natural community having similarities with both prairies and fens, and characterized by a constant supply of calcareous groundwater. Soils are primarily organic (peat), which distinguish prairie fens from true prairies, which always occur on mineral soil composed of sand, silt, and clay.

Prescribed burn: a fire intentionally ignited by trained natural resource professionals according to a specific plan, including the area to be burned, the amount of equipment and personnel needed to manage the fire, and weather parameters that allow for adequate control of flames and smoke, such as humidity, temperature, wind speed, and wind direction. Used as a land management tool to harness the ecological benefits of fire while minimizing the risk of uncontrolled wildfire.

Refugia: microhabitats or areas in which a sensitive species can persist following a disturbance, such as a prescribed fire, in the remainder of the habitat.

Remnant: a small portion of a formerly larger natural community or ecosystem that is relatively unaltered and still retains some or all of its structural and functional characteristics.

S-rank: the numerical rank given to a species or natural community to describe its rarity on a statewide basis. Ranges from 1 to 5, with 1 being extremely rare and 5 being very common.

Savanna: a generic term describing a natural community intermediate between a prairie and a forest, dominated by grasses and broad-leaved herbaceous plants, but also having a partial canopy (5–60 percent) of trees.

Serotinous: a pinecone or other seed case that requires heat from a fire to open and release the seed.

Shifting landscape mosaic: a dynamic process of natural communities in a given area changing spatially over time in response to naturally fluctuating environmental factors such as climate and fire frequency.

Special concern: a species thought to potentially be rare and tracked on a watch list to determine if it should be legally protected as threatened or endangered. Special concern species have no legal protection unless covered under another law pertaining to a particular taxa group (e.g., turtles).

Supercanopy: a large tree with a height significantly greater than the surrounding canopy in a mature forest; in Michigan, usually a white pine or red pine.

Terrestrial: a generic term referring to species or natural communities normally found on land as opposed to water.

Threatened: a species or community that is rare and may become endangered, either statewide (state threatened), nationally (federally threatened), or globally (globally threatened). Usually refers to a species legally protected from intentional destruction on an official list, as designated by a state or federal authority. When used to refer to a natural community or ecosystem, it implies rarity but not legal protection.

Transpire: to give off water vapor through pores in the surface of a plant leaf.

Tufa: a soft rocklike deposit consisting primarily of calcium carbonate, usually formed in lakes or springs as minerals precipitate out of the water.

Warm-season grass: a grass that completes most of its growth during late summer. Examples include many native prairie grasses such as big bluestem, little bluestem, Indian grass, and switchgrass.

Wildfire: an unplanned fire in a natural setting. Wildfires may be of natural origin, such as lightning strikes, or of human origin, such as campfires, burn barrels, discarded cigarette butts, or, rarely, prescribed burns that escape containment lines.

Woodland: a generic term describing a natural community intermediate between a savanna and forest, usually having a canopy between 50 and 80 percent.

Bibliography

Abrams, M. D. 1992. Fire and the Development of Oak Forests. *BioScience* 42:346–353.

Albert, D. A. 1995. Regional Landscape Ecosystems of Michigan, Minnesota, and Wisconsin: A Working Map and Classification. Gen. Tech. Rep. NC-178. St. Paul, Minn.: U.S. Department of Agriculture, Forest Service, North Central Forest Experiment Station.

Albert D. A., and M. A. Kost. 1998. Natural Community Abstract for Lakeplain Wet Prairie. Lansing: Michigan Natural Features Inventory.

———. 1998. Natural Community Abstract for Lakeplain Wet-Mesic Prairie. Lansing: Michigan Natural Features Inventory.

Anderson, R. C., and M. L. Bowles. 1999. Deep-Soil Savannas and Barrens of the Midwestern United States. In *Savannas, Barrens, and Rock Outcrop Plant Communities of North America*, ed. R. C. Anderson, J. S. Fralish, and J. M. Baskin, 155–170. New York: Cambridge University Press.

Apfelbaum, S. I., and A. W. Haney. 1991. Management of Degraded Oak Savanna Remnants in the Upper Midwest: Preliminary Results from Three Years of Study. *Proceedings Oak Woods Management Workshop*, 81–89.

Brown, E. L. 1881. The Old Pioneer, or Forty Years Ago. *Michigan Pioneer and Historical Collections* 3:542.

Case, F. W., and R. B. Case. 1997. *Trilliums*. Portland, Ore.: Timber Press.

Chapman, K. A. 1984. An Ecological Investigation of Native Grassland in Southern Lower Michigan. M.A. thesis, Western Michigan University.

Chapman, K. A. and R. Brewer. 2008. Prairie and Savanna in Southern Lower Michigan: History, Classification, Ecology. *The Michigan Botanist* 47:1–48.

Cohen, J. G. 2000. Natural Community Abstract for Oak-Pine Barrens. Lansing: Michigan Natural Features Inventory.

———. 2001. Natural Community Abstract for Lakeplain Oak Openings. Lansing: Michigan Natural Features Inventory.

———. 2001. Natural Community Abstract for Oak Barrens. Lansing: Michigan Natural Features Inventory.

———. 2004. Natural Community Abstract for Bur Oak Plains. Lansing: Michigan Natural Features Inventory.

———. 2004. Natural Community Abstract for Oak Openings. Lansing: Michigan Natural Features Inventory.

Comer, P. J. 1996. Natural Community Abstract for Pine Barrens. Lansing: Michigan Natural Features Inventory.

Comer, P. J., D. A. Albert, H. A. Wells, B. L. Hart, J. B. Raab, D. L. Price, D. M. Kashian, R. A. Corner, and D. W. Schuen. 1995a. Michigan's Presettlement Vegetation, as Interpreted from the General Land Office Surveys 1816–1856. Lansing: Michigan Natural Features Inventory. Digital map.

Comer, P. J., W. A. MacKinnon, M. L. Rabe, D. L. Cuthrell, M. R. Penskar, and D. A. Albert. 1995b. A Survey of Lakeplain Prairie in Michigan. Report to Michigan Department of Natural Resources, Land and Water Management Division, Coastal Zone Management Program. Report No. 1995-08. Lansing: Michigan Natural Features Inventory.

Copeland, T. E., W. Sluis, and H. F. Howe. 2002. Fire Season and Dominance in an Illinois Tallgrass Prairie Restoration. *Restoration Ecology* 10:315–323.

Coppedge, B. R., D. M. Engle, C. S. Teopfer, and J. H. Shaw. 1998. Effects of Seasonal Fire, Bison Grazing and Climatic Variation on Tallgrass Prairie Vegetation. *Plant Ecology* 139:235–246.

Courteau, J. B. 2005. Direct, Indirect, and Interacting Effects of Overabundant Deer and Invasive Autumn-Olive on Native Vegetation. Ph.D. diss., University of Michigan.

Curtis, J. T. 1959. *Vegetation of Wisconsin: An Ordination of Plant Communities*. Madison: University of Wisconsin Press.

Cuthrell, D. L., P. J. Higman, M. R. Penskar, and J. L. Windus. 1999. The Pollinators of Ohio and Michigan Populations of Eastern Prairie Fringed Orchid (*Platanthera leucophaea*). Report No. 1999-08. Lansing: Michigan Natural Features Inventory.

Czarapata, E. J. 2005. *Invasive Plants of the Upper Midwest: An Illustrated Guide to Their Identification and Control*. Madison: University of Wisconsin Press.

Day, G. M. 1953. The Indian as an Ecological Factor in the Northeast Forest. *Ecology* 34:329–346.

Dunbar, W. 1959. *Kalamazoo and How It Grew*. Kalamazoo: Western Michigan University.

Eagle, A. C., E. M. Hay-Chmielewski, K. T. Cleveland, A. L. Derosier, M. E. Herbert, and R. A. Rustem, eds. 2005. Michigan's Wildlife Action Plan. Lansing: Michigan Department of Natural Resources.

Ellsworth, J. W., and B. C. McComb. 2003. Potential Effects of Passenger Pigeon Flocks on the Structure and Composition of Presettlement Forests of Eastern North America. *Conservation Biology* 17:1548–1558.

Farrand, W. R. 1998. The Glacial Lakes around Michigan. Michigan Department of Environmental Quality, Geological Survey Division, Bulletin 4.

Fuller, G. N., ed. 1928. *Geological Reports of Douglass Houghton—First State Geologist of Michigan 1837–1845*. Lansing: Michigan Historical Commission.

Gustafson, D. J., D. J. Gibson, and D. L Nickrent. 2005. Using Local Seeds in Prairie Restoration Data Support the Paradigm. *Native Plants Journal* 6:25–28.

Hansen, M. F., R. T. Fernandez, and M. R. Penskar. 2007. Wildfire-Resistant Landscape Plants for Michigan. Extension Bulletin E-2948. East Lansing: Michigan State University Extension.

Harding, J. H. 1997. *Amphibians and Reptiles of the Great Lakes Region*. Ann Arbor: University of Michigan Press.

Hoffman, C. F. 1835. A Winter in the West. *Michigan History Magazine* 9:221–228, 413–437.

Howe, H. F. 1994. Response of Early- and Late-Flowering Plants to Fire Season in Experimental Prairies. *Ecological Applications* 4:121–133.

———. 1995. Succession and Fire Season in Experimental Prairie Plantings. *Ecology* 76:1917–1925.

Hubbard, B. 1881. A Michigan Geological Expedition in 1837. *Michigan Pioneer Collections*, vol. 3. Lansing, Mich.: W. S. George.

Kay, C. E. 1995. Aboriginal Overkill and Native Burning: Implications for Modern Ecosystem Management. *Western Journal of Applied Forestry* 10:121–126.

Kline, V. M. 1997. Orchards of Oak and a Sea of Grass. In *The Tallgrass Restoration Handbook for Prairies, Savannas and Woodlands*, ed. S. Packard and C. F. Mutel, 3–21. Washington, D.C.: Island Press.

Knapp, A. K., J. M. Blair, J. M. Briggs, S. L. Collins, D. C. Hartnett, L. C. Johnson, and E. G. Towne. 1999. The Keystone Role of Bison in North American Tallgrass Prairie. *BioScience* 49:39–50.

Kost, M. A. 2004. Natural Community Abstract for Dry Sand Prairie. Lansing: Michigan Natural Features Inventory.

———. 2004. Natural Community Abstract for Dry-Mesic Prairie. Lansing: Michigan Natural Features Inventory.

———. 2004. Natural Community Abstract for Mesic Prairie. Lansing: Michigan Natural Features Inventory.

Kost, M. A., D. A. Albert, J. G. Cohen, B. S. Slaughter, R. K. Schillo, C. R. Weber, and K. A. Chapman. 2007. Natural Communities of Michigan: Classification and Description. Report No. 2007-21. Lansing: Michigan Natural Features Inventory.

Kurta, A. 1995. *Mammals of the Great Lakes Region*. Ann Arbor: University of Michigan Press.

Leach, M. K., and T. J. Givnish. 1996. Ecological Determinants of Species Loss in Remnant Prairies. *Science* 273:1555–1558.

———. 1999. Gradients in the Composition, Structure and Diversity of Remnant Oak Savannas in Southern Wisconsin. *Ecological Monographs* 69:353–374.

Lesica, P., and F. W. Allendorf. 1999. Ecological Genetics and the Restoration of Plant Communities: Mix or Match? *Restoration Ecology* 7:42–50.

Martin, A. C., H. S. Zim, and A. L. Nelson. 1951. *American Wildlife and Plants: A Guide to Wildlife Food Habits*. New York: Dover.

McPherson, G. R. 1997. *Ecology and Management of North American Savannas.* Tuscon: University of Arizona Press.

Minc, L. D., and D. A. Albert. 1990. Oak-Dominated Communities of Southern Lower Michigan: Floristic and Abiotic Comparisons. Unpublished manuscript. Lansing: Michigan Natural Features Inventory.

Mlot, C. 1990. Restoring the Prairie. *BioScience* 40:804–809.

Moon, J. W., R. Wildermuth, J. O. Veatch, C. H. Wonser, B. E. Musgrave, and J. A. Porter. 1932. *Soil Survey of Branch County, Michigan.* Washington, D.C.: U.S. Department of Agriculture, Bureau of Chemistry and Soil Series.

Nielsen, M. C. 1999. *Michigan Butterflies and Skippers: A Field Guide and Reference.* East Lansing: Michigan State University Extension.

Noss, R. F., E. T. LaRoe, and J. M. Scott. 1995. Endangered Ecosystems of the United States: A Preliminary Assessment of Loss and Degradation. National Biological Service Biological Report 28. Washington, D.C.: U.S. Department of the Interior.

Nuzzo, V. 1986. Extent and Status of Midwest Oak Savanna: Presettlement and 1985. *Natural Areas Journal* 6:6–36.

O'Connor, R. 2006. A Land Manager's Guide to Prairies and Savannas in Michigan: History, Classification and Management. Report No. 2006-18. Lansing: Michigan Natural Features Inventory.

Olson, D. M., and E. Dinerstein. 1998. The Global 200: A Representation Approach to Conserving the Earth's Most Biologically Valuable Ecoregions. *Conservation Biology* 12:502–515.

Packard, S. 1988. Just a Few Oddball Species: Restoration and the Rediscovery of the Tallgrass Savanna. *Restoration and Management Notes* 6:13–22.

———. 1993. Restoring Oak Ecosystems. *Restoration and Management Notes* 11:5–16.

Packard, S., and C. F. Mutel, eds. 1997. *The Tallgrass Restoration Handbook for Prairies, Savannas, and Woodlands*. Washington, D.C.: Island Press.

Panzer, R. 2003. Importance of In Situ Survival, Recolonization, and Habitat Gaps in the Postfire Recovery of Fire-Sensitive Prairie Insect Species. *Natural Areas Journal* 23:14–21.

Penskar, M., and P. Higman. 2000. Special Plant Abstract for *Platanthera leucophaea* (Eastern Prairie Fringed Orchid). Lansing: Michigan Natural Features Inventory.

Petersen, S. M., and P. B. Drewa. 2006. Did Lightning-Initiated Growing Season Fires Characterize Oak-Dominated Ecosystems of Southern Ohio? *Journal of the Torrey Botanical Society* 133:217–224.

Peterson, D. W., and P. B. Reich. 2001. Prescribed Fire in Oak Savanna: Fire Frequency Effects on Stand Structure and Dynamics. *Ecological Applications* 11:914–927.

Rabe, M. L. 2001. Special Animal Abstract for *Lycaeides melissa samuelis* (Karner Blue). Lansing: Michigan Natural Features Inventory.

Richburg, J. A. 2005. Timing Treatments to the Phenology of Root Carbohydrate Reserves to Control Woody Invasive Plants. Ph.D. diss., University of Massachusetts.

Rodewald, A. D. 2003. Decline of Oak Forests and Implications for Forest Wildlife Conservation. *Natural Areas Journal* 23: 368–371.

Schmidt, K. A., and C. J. Whelan. 1999. Effects of Exotic *Lonicera* and *Rhamnus* on Songbird Nest Predation. *Conservation Biology* 13:1502–1506.

Short, H. L. 1976. Composition and Squirrel Use of Acorns of Black and White Oak Groups. *Journal of Wildlife Management* 40:479–483.

Southeast Michigan Council of Governments (SEMCOG). 2002. Historic Populations and Employment by Minor Civil Division, Southeast Michigan. Detroit, Michigan. http://library.semcog.org/InmagicGenie/DocumentFolder/HistoricalPopulationSEMI.pdf.

Sparks, J. C., R. E. Masters, D. M. Engle, M. W. Palmer, and G. A. Bukenhofer. 1998. Effects of Late Growing-Season and Late Dormant-Season Prescribed Fire on Herbaceous Vegetation in Restored Pine-Grassland Communities. *Journal of Vegetation Science* 9:133–142.

Spieles, J. B., P. J. Comer, D. A. Albert, and M. A. Kost. 1999. Natural Community Abstract for Prairie Fen. Lansing: Michigan Natural Features Inventory.

Steen, D. A., M. J. Aresco, S. G. Beilke, B. W. Compton, E. P. Condon, C. K. Dodd, H. Forrester, J. W. Gibbons, J. L. Greene, G. Johnson, T. A. Langen, M. J. Oldham, D. N. Oxier, R. A. Saumure, F. W. Schueler, J. M. Sleeman, L. L. Smith, J. K. Tucker, and J. P. Gibbs. 2006. Relative Vulnerability of Female Turtles to Road Mortality. *Animal Conservation* 9:269–273.

Stout, A. B. 1946. The Bur Oak Openings of Southern Wisconsin. *Transactions of the Wisconsin Academy of Sciences, Arts, and Letters* 36:141–161.

Trager, J. C. 1998. An Introduction to Ants (*Formicidae*) of the Tallgrass Prairie. *Missouri Prairie Journal* 18:4–8.

U.S. Fish and Wildlife Service. 2007. Indiana Bat (*Myotis sodalis*) Draft Recovery Plan: First Revision. Minnesota: Fort Snelling.

Van Buren, A. D. P. 1884. Pioneer Annals and Early Settlers of Calhoun County. *Michigan Pioneer and Historical Collections* 5:237–259.

Weir, T. L., H. P. Bais, and J. M. Vivanco. 2003. Intraspecific and Interspecific Interactions Mediated by a Phytotoxin, (–)-Catechin, Secreted by the Roots of *Centaurea maculosa* (Spotted Knapweed). *Journal of Chemical Ecology* 29:2397–2412.

Wilcove, D. S., D. Rothstein, J. Dubow, A. Phillips, and E. Losos. 1998. Quantifying Threats to Imperiled Species in the United States. *BioScience* 48:607–615.

Will-Wolf, S., and F. Stearns. 1999. Dry Soil Oak Savanna in the Great Lakes Region. In *Savannas, Barrens, and Rock Outcrop Plant Communities of North America*, ed. R. C. Anderson, J. S. Fralish, and J. M. Baskin, 135–154. New York: Cambridge University Press.